Controller's Handbook

a Wolters Kluwer business

2nd Edition

Nick A. Shepherd
FCMC, CGA, FCCA

CCH Canadian Limited
300-90 Sheppard Avenue East
Toronto Ontario
M2N 6X1
1 800 268 4522
www.cch.ca

D1458042

Published by CCH Canadian Limited

Important Disclaimer: This publication is sold with the understanding that (1) the authors and editors are not responsible for the results of any actions taken on the basis of information in this work, nor for any errors or omissions; and (2) the publisher is not engaged in rendering legal, accounting or other professional services. The publisher, and the authors and editors, expressly disclaim all and any liability to any person, whether a purchaser of this publication or not, in respect of anything and of the consequences of anything done or omitted to be done by any such person in reliance, whether whole or partial, upon the whole or any part of the contents of this publication. If legal advice or other expert assistance is required, the services of a competent professional person should be sought.

Library and Archives Canada Cataloguing in Publication

Shepherd, Nick
Controller's handbook / Nick A. Shepherd. — 2nd ed.

ISBN 978-1-55367-962-2

1. Controllership — Handbooks, manuals, etc. 2. Business enterprises — Finance — Handbooks, manuals, etc. 3. Corporations — Finance — Handbooks, manuals, etc. I. Title.

HG4027.35.S43 2008   658.15   C2008-906334-1

ISBN 978-1-55367-962-2

© 2008, CCH Canadian Limited

Typeset by CCH Canadian Limited.
Printed in the United States of America.

TABLE OF CONTENTS

Chapter 1

Introduction

Summary ☞

Controllership is a multi-dimensional title that can mean many things. This chapter defines the breadth of controllership in public- and private-sector organizations, and then develops success factors for the position. This includes the importance of balancing time between managing day-to-day accounting activities and ensuring adequate time for effective functioning as a key member of the management team. This chapter shows how a typical controllership position evolves as an organization grows and becomes more complex, and what to expect at each stage of growth. Ethics is a key aspect of a professional financial manager's role, and this chapter summarizes the main components to be considered by a controller in linking ethical management with internal controls and the sustaining of an organization's intangible assets. The chapter concludes with a framework based on PDCA (Plan, Do, Check, and Act), which forms an excellent basis for effective controllership.

Purpose of the *Controller's Handbook*

This handbook is designed to provide new controllers with a high-level overview of the breadth of their accountability and responsibility. A financial controller is a critical member of an organization's management team. The role is key to bringing quantification and facts to discussions surrounding the performance management of an organization. Thus, controllers must first understand the reality and context of their business and then determine how their limited time can be used to create the greatest value for the organization. Balancing management of the low-level detail with the high-level decision making will be a continual challenge, no matter what the size or type of organization.

Breadth of Controllership

The financial controller (*comptroller*, Br.), also known as chief accountant or financial comptroller, can be viewed as the linchpin in any organization. This individual is not only responsible for the preparation of the organization's financial statements, he or she very often inherits a host of specialized responsibilities, ranging from human resource management to the management of information technology.

While all financial controllers share a number of functions, each has a unique job in a particular business environment. In a large publicly traded company, the financial controller may be surrounded by a number of staff members with specialized skills. In a typical small or medium-sized enterprise (SME), the financial controller may have only a few administrative staff with general skills.

The roles, accountabilities, and responsibilities of a financial controller will vary. Typically, the following attributes will affect work responsibilities:

- Public or private company
- Small, medium or large company
- Owner-operated or arm's length management
- Service or manufacturing
- Local, national, or global
- Public or private sector

Within these categories, a controller can be a "one-person show" where everything administrative (i.e., not only accounting but human resource management, information technology management, and all other administration) is handled by either the controller alone or with a small staff. It can expand to a situation where the controller has much narrower responsibilities limited to just part of the overall financial function (e.g., technology, treasury, and other core functions may report up through other specialists). It is important, therefore, that in planning their work assignments, controllers fully understand the unique scope and breadth of their specific situation, and then plan their work within this context.

This guide attempts to describe the range of functions that fall under the jurisdiction of the financial controller in the SME environment. In most small and medium-sized enterprises, there may be no external board, decision making and control are vested with the owners, and resources are limited, so the financial controller will face a number of interesting challenges. In fact, given the scope of the activities and expectations placed on their management skills, a better job title for financial controllers today might be "General Manager and Accountant". Many of the financial controller's tasks in an SME have more to do with overall management than simple accounting.

Many of the topics broached in this handbook may warrant further discussion. This guide focuses on some practical ways to address the challenges and exercise sound financial controllership in the SME environment.

Evolution of the Accounting Tasks in an Organization

Organizations tend to mature along a growth curve that has five clearly defined phases similar to the stages of life.

PHASE	DESCRIPTION AND IMPACT ON THE ROLE OF THE FINANCIAL CONTROLLER
Birth and infancy	• entrepreneur plus family or minimal staff • no financial controller • no defined accounting area; accounts are made up from cash records • financial statements are prepared by a public practitioner in conjunction with the personal income taxes of the owners

PHASE	DESCRIPTION AND IMPACT ON THE ROLE OF THE FINANCIAL CONTROLLER
Childhood	• accounting functions related to cash flow (deposits, invoicing, AP) are delegated to family members or staff • family members or staff each fill a number of roles within the organization • a public practitioner may be consulted for advice • an external bookkeeping service may be used on a contract basis • financial statements are prepared by a public practitioner in conjunction with the personal income taxes of the owners
Adolescence	• there is a sufficient number of accounting transactions to justify delegating them to one or two individuals on a full-time basis • the owners contract with or hire a part-time financial controller • the financial controller focuses on implementing processes but may also be required to handle day-to-day administrative activities • financial statements are prepared by a financial controller and examined by a public practitioner in conjunction with the personal income taxes of the owners
Young adulthood	• there is an internal accounting department but duties may not be fully segregated • the financial controller administers and reviews the activities of the accounting department while handling day-to-day transactions • the financial controller focuses on implementing formal policies and procedures, and control features • monthly or quarterly financial statements are prepared internally and reviewed by the financial controller. Annual financial statements may be reviewed or audited by a public practitioner
Maturity	• there is an internal accounting department with full segregation of duties • the financial controller administers and reviews the work of the accounting department • the financial controller focuses on management issues • consultants provide specialist knowledge in areas such as treasury, tax management, risk management, and IT systems • monthly or quarterly financial statements are prepared internally and reviewed by the financial controller. Annual financial statements are reviewed or audited by a public practitioner

The growth model above shows how the functions of the financial controller will be determined by the organization's current phase of development. For example, it would be very unusual for a financial controller to be in place at the birth/infancy phase of an SME's development, but in most cases, one would be on board at the adolescent phase or later.

Issues to watch for

At the adolescent stage, an organization will have minimal processes in place, and the owner or manager will typically hold most controls personally. The challenge for the new controller is to bring the day-to-day accounting under control, which will probably involve the implementation of a basic PC-based accounting system. Other internal controls should be developed gradually, in line with the expectations of the owner, whose concern will be excessive bureaucracy.

By the time an organization reaches young adulthood, the basic accounting system and processes should be in place, and the focus will turn to building effective controls around financial management. The primary focus will probably be cash-flow management and control (regular forecasts), supported by effective operational processes that support purchasing, receipts and payments, order entry and acceptance (credit), and billing and collections. Payroll processes should be in place, even though there may be a desire to segregate "executive" (especially shareholder/owner) payroll and that for all other staff.

At maturity, the core processes and controls should be in place to manage day-to-day activities. At this stage, a controller will be working with the owner of the business to start broadening areas such as purchasing authority and other operational controls to other staff. Focus will also start to move to areas of business and financial planning, and more analytical (value added) reporting to support operational decisions. Even at this stage, control systems, such as evaluation of capital asset additions, may still remain elusive. Each situation will vary, and the controller will be working very closely with the owner or business-unit manager to ensure the maturity of the controllership function matches the needs of the business.

For the purposes of the discussion in this guide, we will assume that the organization in question is an SME and that it is in the mature phase.

From Accountant to Controller

Accountants making the move to controllership face a significant challenge. Many entrepreneurs traditionally see the need for accounting as a non-value added activity where the absolute minimum resources should be assigned. Success in demonstrating value to the entrepreneur and other managers will come less from pure accounting abilities as it will from being an effective member of the management team and contributing positively to the overall development of the organization.

Building skill sets in areas such as planning, reporting, and relationship building will become more important than staying fully up to date with tax legislation or being able to maintain the computer network.

Typical Functions of Controllership

One could argue that there is no typical financial controllership role, but there are activities and processes that appear common to most organizations.

The following chart shows a well-proven model for management that will form the basis for our discussion of the controller's role contained within the following chapters. It is often referred to as the PDCA model (Plan, Do, Check, and Act), as it sets up a continual loop for defining what you want to achieve; setting up and executing activities to make desired results happen; establishing a measurements system so that you can assess progress against your plans; and, finally, using that information to take action, either to correct the situation (if progress is not tracking to plan) or possibly to amend the plans. One of the challenges that will be addressed is "how much time should controllers assign to each of these core activities in order to execute their role effectively?"

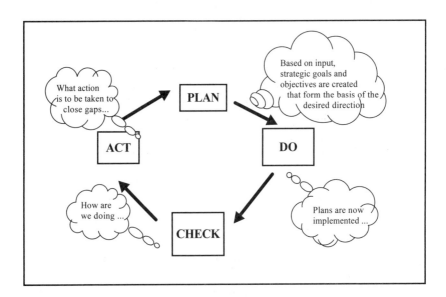

Planning — deciding what you want to achieve

Nothing is achieved without a plan. The controller's role in planning will involve working with owners to develop a business plan that defines what the organization is trying to achieve. This step will involve consultation with owners and other stakeholders; assessment of current status, expectations, and direction; and establishment of clear business plans. Once they are in place, the more traditional areas of developing financial plans will follow. Controllers must ensure that their focus on planning includes both the organizational-level activity as well as plans for their own functional areas of responsibility. In addition, core business objectives developed at this stage must have outcome measures attached to them so that progress can be tracked. A controller must ensure, through his or her knowledge of the organization, that these measures reflect those "critical few" that are focused, concise, and key to achievement of the organization's business goals. These are often called KPIs or Key Performance Indicators.

Doing — executing the plan

Based on decisions made at the planning stage, the financial controller should then focus on identifying and making best use of all of the organization's resources; that is, how to allocate the organization's money. This involves exercising the management role by looking at the overall organization, as well as by being head of accounting and running all of the financial management processes. Every organization achieves its business objectives through processes and projects. The controller must ensure that every business objective established at the planning stage has been "decomposed" into specific executable strategies, plans, and actions that have both clear accountability and are supported by operational performance measures to track ongoing progress.

This aspect includes being concerned about efficiency, effectiveness, and adequate control; the effective controller will view all of these aspects through both the accounting perspective as well as a practical organizational management perspective. The controller should be as objective about the resources consumed in their own accounting "factory" as they are about the organization's overall use of resources.

Relationship building and people management

In addition to overseeing revenues and expenditures, the controller will generally be called upon to manage human resources and to maintain key relationships internally and externally.

Nothing is achieved in any organization without the active involvement and participation of people. In the 21st century, where service organizations, intellectual capital, and knowledge management are all becoming increasingly important, this aspect of the controller's role is growing. Effective controllers will place a heavy emphasis on developing their skill sets in this area, often referred to as the "soft skills".

Checking — ensuring your plans are being achieved

Performance measurement is a critical step in effective management. Controllers must ensure that the performance measurement system contains both tracking of the outcomes defined in the plans as well as tracking of activities that are being executed in order to achieve these plans. Such measures should contain both financial and non-financial metrics that represent the key dimensions required to achieve the organization's desired outcomes. This typically includes traditional "outcome/after the fact" financial measurements (supplemented by metrics related to clients or customers), internal process performance determinants, project status reporting, and employee development aspects such as learning, improvement, morale, and others.

Role of information technology in reporting

Controllers must ensure that the organization recognizes the importance of, and implements, state-of-the-art technology to manage the key data relative to execution of the business activities. Information is the life blood of today's organization, and an integrated, seamless system is key to rapid recognition of performance issues and limitation of excessive transaction-processing costs. While building a business case for such investments, the controller will need to recognize the strategic importance of timely and accurate decision making in today's fast-paced and rapidly changing economic environment; additionally, consideration must be given to the need to provide staff with the right tools to do their jobs effectively and cost efficiently. This may require understanding and analysis of organization-wide staff activities in order to identify the excess costs being incurred where effective information management is not in place.

Acting — using performance measures to deliver results

Finally, the controller must ensure that performance reports lead to action. The final stage of the performance loop is to ensure that report information is available to those who need assurance that they are achieving plans, or leads to decisions as to how to respond when gaps are appearing between planned outcomes and reality.

Modern Controllership in the Public Sector

While this handbook focuses on the role of a controller within an SME, many of the skills discussed are equally important in any type of organization. The public sector is undertaking a major renewal initiative that not only repositions the role of financial management, but also expands the responsibility for stewardship and many other traditional aspects of effective controllership across all levels of management.

Modern controllership focuses on changing the role of managers in the public sector so that they become more involved and accountable in the areas of financial management. Areas of defined learning and improvement include: improving the responsible stewardship of resources through effective departmental planning and work execution; ensuring effective controls through adequate reporting and analysis against plans; and focusing on areas such as ethics of staff, effective risk assessment of alternative courses of action, and the potential financial impact of key decisions. Controllers and financial managers in equivalent roles in the public sector need to ensure that they understand the changing expectations of line management and structure, and organize their financial data collection, reporting, analysis, and support in ways that complement the changing needs of these individuals.

While this handbook does not try to cover these aspects or deal with the unique features of the controller in a public service setting, all controllers can benefit from a review of the skills that make up the framework for modern controllership in order to develop their personal skill sets.[1]

In addition, all controllers should strive, through their role as members of any management team, to develop similar understandings of financial management aspects from all other managers. The controller cannot provide iron-clad control systems, and much of his or her success will rest upon the values, integrity, and understanding of effective management skills of other members of the organization's management team.

Time Management for the Controller

For a controller, time is the scarcest resource. Planning, managing resources, and reporting all take time; all of these aspects, as well as taking action, require the management of human resources — both internal and external. This requires that controllers also invest time in the relationship aspects of their position — in fact, this may be THE most important factor for success in moving from an accounting manager to a broad-based and effective controller.

---

[1] For more information see Federal Government of Canada, Treasury Board website at http://www.tbs-sct.gc.ca/cmo_mfc/resources2_e.asp.

The following table illustrates how a financial controller employed by an SME in the mature phase might allocate time to various functions. Note that percentages and equivalent weeks spent on each aspect of the job will vary depending on the type of controllership position. The more senior the position, the less time would be spent on process management and detailed work in the measurement area, and the more on planning and relationship building. Controllers should establish their own schedules, based on the total annual hours they anticipate working, by determining a combination of time that comprehensively includes the minimum in each of the areas shown. Care MUST be taken not to spend too much time in details, as this will result in limiting the controller's ability to add real value to the business through becoming a partner in effective decision making.

PDCA	Activities	Time spent	Annual time
Plan	Planning activity of all types	10%–25%	5–12 weeks
Do	Process management	20%–50%	10–24 weeks
	Developing/managing relationships	15%–25%	7–12 weeks
Check	Measuring and monitoring	10%–15%	5–7 weeks
Act	Analysis and action support	10%–20%	5–10 weeks

The financial controller who is adding true value to the organization will be allocating time in all four areas. Unfortunately, many financial controllers tend to focus on their area of resource management (accounting), and on reporting and information management; they allocate too little time to planning management, and people and relationship management.

To repeat: the successful financial controller is one who has learned to allocate the time to be involved in all four key management areas. The easiest way to do so is to delegate a portion of the activities. Guidelines are included in the chart on the following page.

This chart, and the ones that follow in subsequent sections, attempt to identify approaches that controllers might take to unburden some of the detailed work and allow them to focus more on the higher-value, business-support activities. In every aspect of the role, controllers should be thinking "how can I delegate this work to others?" so they can use their own time to contribute effectively to organizational management.

RESPONSIBILITIES TO DELEGATE TO STAFF	CORE RESPONSIBILITIES OF THE FINANCIAL CONTROLLER	RESPONSIBILITIES TO DELEGATE TO A CONSULTANT
• delegate when it is more cost-effective for staff to perform the activity	• provide expertise in general management and accounting • provide support to the owner	• contract out when it is more cost-effective to hire a consultant to provide specialized knowledge or skills
Tasks may include: • routine transactions and administration • generation of routine reports • routine communication with external bodies	Tasks may include: • monitoring, analysis, and interpretation • implementation of policies and procedures • coaching and mentoring of managers and supervision of accounting department staff • support to the owner • liaison with external stakeholders • planning	

Financial controllers in organizations in the mature phase do not add value when they perform activities on the left-hand side of the table. However, in the case of an organization which is in the adolescent phase and has limited resources to spare, it may be necessary for the financial controller to assume some of the duties listed in the left-hand column.

Note that in most organizations, financial controllers do not add value when they perform activities on the right-hand side of the table either. While it may be tempting for them to invest the time to acquire specialized knowledge so that they can take on additional duties in the right-hand column, from the owner's point of view, it may cost less to hire a specialist on a contract basis.

Effective controllers find a way to manage this challenge and achieve a balance in their lives while at the same time executing their professional work effectively. This starts with ensuring that there is a plan in place supported by an understanding of where time is currently being allocated. Using this and identifying the gap between the two, the controller can start to plan his or her work, delegate, and set priorities. Failure to do this can result in high stress levels, missed deadlines, and deteriorating relationships with owners and other key members of the controller's team.

While no time management system is ever perfect, controllers should adopt some type of plan in order to execute the remainder of the activities outlined in this handbook in a way that provides value to the organization. Included in Appendix II of the handbook are examples of two charts that can help identify where time is currently being spent and help to create an improvement plan (see Exhibits 1–A and 1–B).

Ethics and the Financial Controller

One of the key values of professional accreditation is the personal and collective commitment to live and make decisions in a manner that upholds an agreed code of ethics (often called a Code of Conduct and other variations). In recent years, highly public financial scandals have cast suspicion on how both managers and professionals conduct themselves in their business and personal activities.

A controller must consider three legs of the ethical "stool".

First, controllers, as professionally designated individuals, must conduct themselves in accordance with their organization's Code of Ethical Conduct. They must know this code, what the implications are for their position, and how to deal with problems and issues that appear to be in conflict with the code. This typically means following a fairly well-defined process to assess the situation and ensure that all available facts are understood, as well as knowing how to escalate or resolve the situation. However, if resolution is not possible, professionals must be prepared to "draw a line in the sand" and, if need be, remove themselves from the organization. A well-known expression is, "it takes a lifetime to build your professional integrity and reputation but one event or indiscretion to permanently damage or destroy it".

Second, controllers in ethical management must encourage their organization to develop and communicate its own code of ethical conduct in a way that guides the thinking of all employees, from board member on down, as they make their day-to-day decisions. The behaviour of employees in any organization impacts many intangible assets such as reputation, brand, innovation, client satisfaction, supplier relationships, and many others.[2] Topical research indicates that the value of these assets today is growing faster than those on an organization's balance sheet. If a controller is to protect the organization's overall value and ensure continuity and sustainability, then all efforts must be focused on attempting to ensure consistent and acceptable behaviour.

Third, internal controls today depend to a significant degree on the decisions and actions that individual staff members at all levels within an organization take. For a controller to understand and address the controls

---

[2] For more on this topic, see *Governance, Accountability, and Sustainable Development* (2005), by Nick A. Shepherd, published by Thomson Carswell.

required in response to organizational risk, risks associated with unethical behaviour must be addressed. Through new controls in areas such as hiring, education, training, communications, and performance assessment, ethics will be developed that enhance and encourage the type of behaviour that is consistent with a code of conduct. The alternative, increasing the traditional approach to controls, has a tendency to create more bureaucracy and impede an organization's ability to be responsive and agile — key success factors in any organization functioning in today's competitive environment.

Chapter 2

Planning Management

Summary ☞

Effective planning is at the heart of good controllership. This chapter shows how the controller should participate in setting an organizational mission and creating a business plan. It then discusses financial planning for the longer and short term, including budgets and tax planning. Controllers should ensure that effective risk assessment and risk management are included in planning, as this forms the foundation of effective internal controls and links back to effective governance.

15

Planning management is the first group of functions that the financial controller may be responsible for in an SME. This area includes activities such as business and tax planning. While such functions are deemed important, in many SMEs, there is just not enough time for the financial controller to grant them all the attention they deserve. However, planning management is one area where the financial controller can add significant value to the organization.

The following table summarizes the planning management functions and gives a general indication as to how the underlying tasks should be assigned.

Planning Management	Hours Per Year	Assignment of Responsibility
Vision and strategic planning	160	• the controller assists the owners by initiating and facilitating vision and strategic planning
Business planning	200	• staff compiles historical data • the controller develops and reviews policy • consultants may be contacted for forecasting information
Finance and tax planning	135	• staff compiles historical data • the controller develops and reviews policies related to finance and tax planning • consultants are used for tax planning
Risk management	60	• the controller assists the owners in the implementation of risk management • the controller develops and reviews policies governing the risk management process • consultants may be required to provide support
Governance	40	• the controller assists the owners both in identifying and in addressing governance issues

Vision and Strategic Planning

Vision and strategic planning form an important area where the financial controller can add value to the organization. Unfortunately, financial controllers often do not allocate enough time for this vital exercise. While defining the vision of the owner and the mission of the company is critical to the success of the SME, it is often the case that they remain locked up unshared in the owner's mind.

A company's vision and mission statements serve to encapsulate the spirit or essence of the organization, and defining them is a profound exercise that requires deep critical analysis. Once these statements are formalized, they should be communicated to all employees as a guide for their individual activities.

In sum, if the financial controller is to add value under planning management, he must first persuade the owner of the importance of formalizing and sharing the organization's vision and mission.

The next step in the process is to understand the organization as it currently exists and to evaluate where it stands in relation to the business environment. This can easily be accomplished by doing a SWOT analysis, i.e., by identifying the organization's strengths, weaknesses, opportunities, and threats (see Appendix II, Exhibits 2-A and 2-B, for SWOT templates). The SWOT analysis could include a determination of the factors which are critical to providing the organization with a competitive edge. Insights or clues often surface when the organization can identify its key cost and revenue drivers. Within the context of SWOT analysis, the organization can also actively participate in gathering and assimilating information about the business environment, including information on competitors.

After gaining a better understanding of the fundamentals that make the organization tick, the next step is to identify long-term strategic goals (projecting three or more years hence) that will give the organization a strategic advantage. This lays the groundwork for the organization to identify specific activities that will move it towards fulfilling these goals. There is no simple way to identify strategic goals. One method open to the financial controller is to apply the ideas of Michael Porter, a professor at the Harvard School of Business and a leading authority on competitive strategy.[1] Ideally, once the strategic goals have been identified, they should be prioritized.

The following are some vision and strategic planning functions that a financial controller must address.

---

[1] For more on this, see "From Competitive Advantage to Corporate Strategy," *Harvard Business Review*, May/June 1987, pp. 43-59, as well as subsequent publications by Porter.

RESPONSIBILITIES TO BE DELEGATED TO STAFF	CORE RESPONSIBILITIES OF THE FINANCIAL CONTROLLER	RESPONSIBILITIES TO DELEGATE TO A CONSULTANT
• provide input on vision and mission statements when requested	• gain the support of the owner to formalize the organization's vision and mission statements	• consider using a facilitator to develop initial vision and mission statements
	• review existing vision and mission statements and revise them if necessary • communicate vision and mission statements to staff	
	• implement a strategic planning process appropriate to the organization	
• understand how one's individual responsibilities are related to the organization's strategic plans	• communicate the results of strategic planning to the owners and staff	
• understand how one's individual performance has contributed to achieving the organization's goals	• at the end of a stated period, review the original strategic plan and compare it with the results obtained to date	

The following are a few key points concerning vision and strategic planning:

- Participation of the owner and the key decision-makers is critical to the successful development of vision and mission statements.

- Do not strive for perfection — vision and strategy statements are tools for setting the tone and giving the overall direction of the firm, not an iron-clad all-inclusive legalistic summary of its *raison d'être*.

- The vision must be based on current performance and be realistic to employees and staff.

- Vision and strategy must be driven by the reality of the market and the business environment — for objectivity and perspective, be sure to solicit external input.

- Good strategy builds on a realistic assessment of strengths and weaknesses.

- Opportunities and threats should be included as a guide to the development of action plans.

- The views of all stakeholders should be investigated and taken into account in developing vision and mission statements.

- Good strategy must include the notion of continual improvement in all areas and activities, and be based on goals that are established through best practices.

- Strategic plans should consider activity centres first — like clients and sales, materials and suppliers, people and training — and be converted only afterwards to financial information: your measures must link your organization's activity to its financial performance.

- Ensuring that your employees everywhere understand the organization's plans and their role in achieving them is the key to realizing your strategic vision and plans.

Business Planning

Business planning connects together the aspirations of the organization as established through the vision and mission statements, the existing reality of the organization's capacity and performance, and the level of resources that can be made available to achieve the plans. Controllers should be cautious about making business planning into a purely financial-based process.

Various models have been developed over the years for planning, and the controller can either adopt one or develop his or her own. It is critical to ensure that there is wide involvement in the process where possible and that the process be driven by the owner and senior management. Communications of the vision, as well as key business goals and objectives, must be in place and clearly communicated as a base upon which to plan.

An example of an effective model for thinking about how to approach planning is shown below.

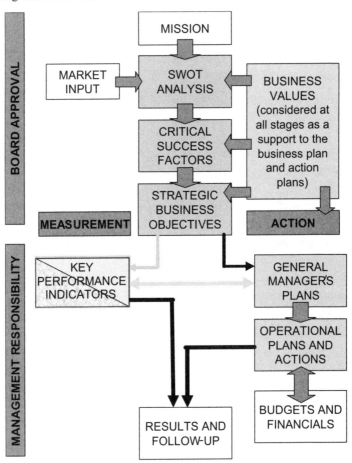

This chart shows that responsibility for planning is typically split between owners or between the Board and management. The Board typically sets the mission, as well as a clear set of corporate values that define organizational conduct (this will typically be the foundation for an organization's ethics policies). The Board then works with the CEO to complete the remaining steps as part of the strategic planning activity. From this comes a clear understanding of what must be addressed in future plans and action (the critical success factors or CSFs) and from these the core business objectives. These then provide the basis for "direction" to management, who builds operating plans capable of delivering the required results.

It is important that whatever the model adopted, standard terminology is used. Opinions may vary but within any organization each manager and every employee must have a common understanding of what the words being used actually mean in their own organization. Key words might include:

- Goals

- Objective

- Strategy

- Strategic Plan

- Action Plan

- Processes and Activities

A suggested example of terminology is included in Exhibit 2-C, Appendix II, as one set of descriptions that could be used.

One of the models that can be used to establish common terminology is shown below and incorporates the concepts of best practice in building a learning organization.

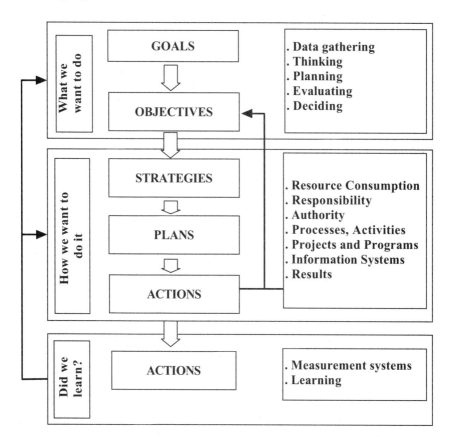

The controller acts mainly in a management advisory role at this stage of planning, ensuring that plans are being made on valid and factual information and that the practical realities of linking desires with resources are being considered.

Once this thinking process has been completed, the controller will now have the task of working with all other managers to convert the proposed "Strategies, Plans, and Actions" into a financial plan that identifies revenues, expenses, and capital investments required to actually execute them. Controllers should be diligent in identifying areas where there are inadequate and/or incomplete plans as to how certain plans and expectations will be achieved. Asking questions such as "where are the resources?" and "who is going to do this?" are critical to ensuring reality within the process.

Financial Planning

Before we discuss issues related to financial planning, it is important to define what kinds of things to include. The following items will be discussed in this section: operational budgeting, capital budgeting, and business plans for projects occurring in the next one to three years. Finance and tax must also be considered under business planning. These will be discussed in the next section.

After formalizing the organization's vision and business plan, the financial controller should be focusing on how best to deploy the organization's resources to facilitate attaining its goals and objectives. Operational and capital budgets are two sets of tools available. Cross-referencing the budgets to the strategic goals of the organization, which have been prioritized, makes it easier to rationalize the allocation of resources. (Note: monitoring the budget alongside the actual expenditure will be discussed under Reporting and Information Management.)

On occasion, the financial controller is required to analyze a potential project and then develop a business plan to support it. In developing such a business plan, he or she must communicate in a concise manner. In addition to describing the critical variables, the business plan must profile the quality and competencies of management.

The following are some key business planning functions that a financial controller must address:

Responsibilities Delegated to Staff	Core Responsibilities of the Financial Controller	Responsibilities Delegated to a Consultant
• compile operational and capital budget data	• integrate operational and capital budgeting processes with the strategic plan	
	• establish policies and procedures related to the operational and capital budgeting processes	
	• analyze and subsequently develop business plans for miscellaneous projects	• the support of consultants may be required

- Ensure that the fundamental assumptions that underlie the plans are agreed upon (market growth, interest rates, etc.).

- Involve staff in the preparation of operational and capital budgets.

- Ensure consistency between the plans and budgets.

- Ensure consistency between capital expenditure plans (to lower costs, etc.) and assumptions concerning savings in the expense plans.

- Compare the current performance to the budget/plan.

- Ensure that the actions that drive the numbers are built into the goals and objectives of the responsible staff members. (Make sure they are not just token "accounting numbers".)

- Communicate the finalized budgets to staff.

- Ensure linkage and alignment — financial goals must be linked to action goals.

- Balance time spent *versus* amount of detail included: "just enough planning" is the target.

The most important role of a controller's position is to ensure reality within the process of planning. This does not mean that owners cannot have ambitious plans — indeed that is the essence of success as an entrepreneur; the key is to ensure the controller is thinking about risk and impact of positions taken, and advising the owners on these aspects. The temptation to just "improve the numbers" without going back and focusing on changes to strategies, plans, or actions MUST be avoided if planning is to be of any value.

Moving beyond the budget

With today's fast-paced and rapidly changing economic environment, an increasing number of organizations are moving away from traditional approaches to budgeting and are seeking and adopting more flexible approaches to short-term financial planning. The more popular approach involves strengthening the focus on organizational strategy and reducing the time spent on annual financial plans — recognizing that in many cases these become obsolete as a control tool soon after they are developed. In place of budgets, organizations are focusing on approaches such as having a current quarter forecast plus a rolling forecast that is four quarters ahead. This provides an effective snapshot of the financial implications of the continued deployment of existing strategies. This approach also includes clear accountability for specific outcomes and results, and a broad-based performance monitoring and measurement system, often referred to as a "corporate dashboard", which is based on the concepts of the "balanced scorecard".[2]

Those wishing to study these trends in more detail should visit the web site of the "Beyond Budgeting Round Table" (BBRT) at www.bbrt.org where extensive details of emerging approaches in this area are constantly being developed and applied in practice.

Tax and Treasury Planning

In this section, the discussion will be limited to finance and tax planning activities that look forward one to three years. The issue of short-term cash management will be discussed under resource management.

A financial controller can add value if he or she is able to structure tax planning activities to maximize cash flows. One obvious strategy is to take appropriate measures to defer taxes as long as possible. A second strategy would be to minimize the assets that are capitalized. Notwithstanding, it is important to understand that, while it is appropriate to arrange the organization's affairs to keep taxes as low as possible, tax evasion activities are illegal and must be avoided.

After the operational and capital budgets are finalized and the organization has identified appropriate measures to minimize taxes, the financial controller can initiate financial forecasting. This will provide the organization with a better understanding of how its performance will be affected by

---

[2] See *The Balanced Scorecard* by Robert S. Kaplan and David P. Norton; Harvard Business Press (1996), as well as *The Execution Premium* by the same authors and publisher (2008).

external variables like interest rates and tax rates, and internal variables like its operational and capital budgets. A key piece of information that financial forecasting will produce is the level of incremental debt and equity financing that the company may require during the next three years.

One last function remains to be discussed under financial planning: once the organization's future requirements for debt and equity are known, the financial controller should initiate, in conjunction with the owner, appropriate plans to secure financing from the banks and from equity investors.

The following are some key tax and financial planning functions that a financial controller must address:

RESPONSIBILITIES DELEGATED TO STAFF	CORE RESPONSIBILITIES OF THE FINANCIAL CONTROLLER	RESPONSIBILITIES DELEGATED TO A CONSULTANT
	• implement tax planning activities to maximize cash flows	• consult a tax specialist
	• develop financial forecasting	
• prepare financial reports	• maintain an appropriate capital structure for the organization	• consult the bank manager and other advisors (e.g., investment counsel)

- Tax planning is not limited to the organization, but must also be extended to the owner's affairs.

- Tax plans should be created and agreed upon in accordance with advice from external advisors.

- The financial controller must be knowledgeable concerning changes in tax regulations.

- The financial forecast should focus on quality of assumptions rather than quantity of data.

- The financial controller must keep investors abreast of future plans and financing requirements.

- The goal of good planning and forecasting is to not be surprised. Running a sensitivity analysis on the main variables is a key part of the exercise.

- Remember, there are alternatives to financing. Balance risk, cost, and flexibility to handle the changes in results that may occur.

- Ensure that key managers are aware of the impact of their actions on financial planning — purchasing (inventory, credit terms), sales (deferred payments, milestones, etc.), and others.

Risk Management

Risk management has traditionally been viewed as "taking care of insurance". While this is still an important aspect, the financial controller must understand that insurance is only one aspect of risk management, and that value can be added if a more comprehensive risk management process is implemented.

First, risk could be defined as "exposure to mischance, exposure to loss, chance of injury or loss...". With this in mind, any generic risk management process should include the following steps:

- identification of risk;

- evaluation/assessment of risk;

- action planning;

  ➤ eliminate risk through changes in operating procedures,

  ➤ minimize risk by implementing "good work practices" including training and audits,

  ➤ transfer risk by taking out insurance (may be 100% or a shared-risk approach),

  ➤ retain or increase risk where the potential loss is small compared to the cost of premiums to transfer it;

- monitoring of risk potential over time, and re-assessment on a regular basis.

It is important to understand that risk management is not just an administrative activity designed to protect assets and minimize risk. Properly implemented, the risk management process can also serve to identify opportunities and to supplement strategic planning activities.

Financial controllers must focus on knowing the business at the operating level: critical thinking processes can then be applied to ensure that potential risks are identified, evaluated, and dealt with.

The following are some key risk management functions that a financial controller must address:

RESPONSIBILITIES DELEGATED TO STAFF	CORE RESPONSIBILITIES OF THE FINANCIAL CONTROLLER	RESPONSIBILITIES DELEGATED TO A CONSULTANT
	• encourage the owner to implement a risk management process as part of the strategic planning process	
• provide input to the risk management process	• implement a risk management process	
	• identify and assess risk	• a consultant may be required to address specialized or complex areas
	• reduce risk	
	• purchase insurance	• consult an insurance broker

There are a number of ways to classify risk. The financial controller might consider the following classifications: structural risk, commercial and operating risk, and other risk.

Structural risk

Risks in this category include changes and/or losses that could affect the organization's ability to stay in business. In many cases, the crucial component is that key personnel maintain their involvement in the business.

Elements that pose a structural risk include:

- changes in ownership;
- changes in key management;
- changes in key technical staff;
- health risk and/or death of key staff;
- risk of key individuals travelling together;

- impact on directors and officers of maintaining legal compliance;

- impact of legislative changes on various areas of the business (national and international);

- impact on key staff of moving the physical location.

Commercial and Operating Risk

This category of risk will be more familiar to most financial controllers, as it covers the areas where insurance is typically involved. Commercial and operating risks that financial controllers should address include:

- risk to tangible assets, such as

  ➢ property, plant, and equipment,

  ➢ inventories,

  ➢ loss of cash (fraud, theft, etc.);

- risk to business continuance (through fire, etc.) over and above asset losses;

- exchange rate/currency exposure and other financial risk (loans/exposure);

- accounts receivable/bad debt risk;

- marketplace risks (product and service liabilities);

- risk of accident to employees at work;

- risk of loss of records (protect electronic data as well as hard copy);

- risk through loss of, or problems with, key suppliers;

- need to take out security bonds on various employees;

- risks of corporate espionage.

Other risk

In addition to the areas identified above, financial controllers should be aware of the risk inherent in other activities in order to limit the organization's exposure. Situations that could create risk of loss or legal liability include the following:

- environmental risk related to pollution, dumping, effluents, employee health hazards, and others;

- warranties and guarantees;

- E&O (Errors and Omissions) — usually in professional services organizations;

- potential for wrongful dismissal action where problems are not documented or inadequate consideration is given;

- miscellaneous liabilities (e.g., lawsuits resulting from serving liquor to individuals at parties or functions who suffer an accident due to impairment).

An example of a risk management checklist has been added to provide a suggested approach to how a controller may build an assessment process to identify where risks exist within the organization they work for (see Exhibit 2-D in Appendix II).

Governance

Governance can be thought of as accountability, and from the point of view of the financial controller, the topic is complex. The role of the financial controller is to ensure that the owner and key decision-makers have policies and procedures in place to ensure that the organization is acting in a responsible manner as concerns all of its stakeholders: owners, employees, customers, suppliers, regulators, tax collecting agencies, and the local community.

The following are some key governance functions that a financial controller must address:

RESPONSIBILITIES DELEGATED TO STAFF	CORE RESPONSIBILITIES OF THE FINANCIAL CONTROLLER	RESPONSIBILITIES DELEGATED TO A CONSULTANT
• timely reporting of key data	• have the owner and key decision-makers systematically identify and discuss key governance issues	• periodic advice/reports on emerging issues
	• develop policies and procedures that address governance issues	
	• train the staff in the application of these policies and procedures	
	• review policies and procedures to ensure that they are current	

- In some organizations, while there may be no formal reason to incur the cost of an audit for governance reasons, it may be appropriate to have one performed on a yearly basis and for the benefit of the various investors.

- Ensure that periodic surveys of key stakeholders, such as clients and employees, are undertaken, and that the feedback obtained is discussed.

- External boards are critically important to effective governance. Make sure that agenda items are in place for Board members to address key governance issues.

- In private organizations, consider using an "Advisory Board" which includes external representation to assess and advise on governance issues.

- With external boards, ensure that representation is broad enough to provide a variety of backgrounds.

- Establish a "critical success factors" checklist for governance issues, and have periodic assessments conducted against it.

- Ensure that the division of roles and responsibilities between Board and management is clear, and that these are cascaded and communicated within the organization.

- Ensure that a code of ethics or equivalent statement is in place that conveys a clear set of principles and values against which actions can be assessed.

- Ensure that reports and observations from any internal or external audits are reviewed and assessed for their impact on the organization and its action plans.

- Ensure that a periodic "risk assessment" on the overall operation of the organization is conducted and includes items such as continuity of ownership, insurance on key personnel, etc.

Public perception of the effectiveness with which governance has been applied has suffered significant setbacks over the last 15 years or so, and, in particular, with recent scandals and fraud charges in some large organizations. While controllers in SME situations may feel that this has less impact on them, it is important that systems and controls are in place to ensure effective compliance with the expectations and values of the owners and other shareholders as well as an operating philosophy that is founded in ethical behavior towards all stakeholders, including society at large.

Risk Management, Governance, and Internal Control

No organization can be effectively governed without those who have responsibility for oversight, planning, and management having a clear understanding of what risks exist, where they are, how likely they are to occur, and what the impact would be if they did occur. Therefore, a broad-based risk assessment MUST be part of effective governance. Such an activity would then allow boards to establish policies around risk management, and from this, the controller would be able to ensure that resources are directed at controls that are required to address the most appropriate area. While the PCAOB (Public Company Accounting Oversight Board) in the US has established clear requirements for risk assessment to meet SOX (Sarbanes-Oxley) legislation, the approach in Canada is more flexible. However, a model such as the US CoSo (Committee of Sponsoring Organizations) framework can provide an effective approach to developing a risk assessment.

In today's 21st century economy, often referred to as the "information society", many of the assets that a controller is responsible for protecting for shareholders and other stakeholders are no longer on the balance sheet but are intangibles. Significant risks to these can occur where, for example, employee actions damage an organization's reputation or its relationships with suppliers, customers, or even internally between employees. Controllers need to ensure that effective risk assessment extends to addressing such items and that controls put in place cover aspects such as the ethical behaviour of employees. This may require shifting "control" resources (such as verifying signatures and checking expense claims) to areas such as pre-employment testing (such as behavioural assessments).

Key Success Factors in Effective Planning

The following checklist can help controllers identify key areas for planning in order to ensure that their organization has addressed the major steps in the process:

Area of concern	OK	NI	NA	NR	Comments
The organization has a clear Mission/Vision					
All employees are aware of the Mission/Vision and their role in its achievement					
Planning is actively led by the most senior management					
There is a clearly defined planning framework and vocabulary					
Senior managers are actively involved in planning and prioritizing					
Employee input is actively sought in identification of issues and developing plans					
The planning framework includes "reality checking" (SWOT analysis, external input)					
The organization has clearly established its critical success factors (CSFs)					
Broad-based performance reporting of current status is available (e.g., people, clients, process, etc.)					
Planning is supported by a clearly defined management accountability framework					
Board/Owners have established a set of core business objectives					
Business objectives are focused and limited (3–5 in total)					
Business objectives are clearly defined and measurable					
Organizational direction and objectives are clearly communicated to ALL employees					

Area of concern	OK	NI	NA	NR	Comments
Each business objective is clearly linked to strategies for execution					
Strategies for execution have clear ownership and are measurable					
Strategies for execution have been adequately resourced (money, people, skills)					
Short-term financial plans are aligned with longer-term business plans					
Short-term financial projections are reviewed/updated on a regular basis					
Short-term execution strategies are embedded in employees' action plans					
Action plans are documented and form part of regular employee reviews					
Achievement of individual plans is linked to employee compensation (incentives)					
Implications of taxation have been incorporated into business plans					
Financing strategies are in place to ensure adequate cash flow					
"What if" simulations have been performed on key assumptions/aspects within the business plan (e.g., currency changes, commodity price changes, etc.)					
A performance measurement system links objectives to action, and reports on activity and outcome					

Note — OK = Acceptable; NI = Needs Improvement; NA= Not Acceptable; NR = Not Relevant

Chapter 3

Execution: Developing and Managing Effective Processes

— **Summary** ☞ —

Most accounting activities are performed using well-defined processes, and this covers the "Doing" aspects of the PDCA management cycle. In this chapter, the concept of effective process management is discussed, and in particular, attention is drawn to the excess costs created by processes that are not well designed or which fail to work correctly 100% of the time. The chapter then looks at each of the core accounting processes and identifies how the controller should seek to delegate the day-to-day routine tasks involved. Finally, aspects of cost management and project management are briefly discussed.

Effective controllers must be able to minimize the time they personally spend doing detailed accounting work. Core accounting processes, such as those shown below, should be delegated wherever possible. While the times shown are general guidelines that each controller must modify to suit his or her own reality, they highlight the importance of focusing the minimum time necessary to ensure the accounting processes remain controlled and effective.

RESOURCE MANAGEMENT	HOURS PER YEAR	ASSIGNMENT OF RESPONSIBILITY
Cash management	155	• day-to-day administration is assigned • the controller establishes policies, monitors the cash position, and maintains internal control
Revenue and AR management	75	• day-to-day administration is assigned • the controller establishes policies and reviews AR
Expense and AP management	60	• day-to-day administration is assigned • the controller establishes policies and reviews AP
Inventory management	60	• day-to-day administration is assigned • the controller establishes policies and reviews inventory
Facilities management	60	• day-to-day administration is assigned • the controller plans for facilities
Other management accounting	varies	• the controller may be required to undertake special management accounting projects • the help of consultants may be required

Concepts and Benefits of Effective Process Management

In recent years, a great deal of attention has been paid to process management. The concept is not new, but it has become recognized as a key building block for many improvement opportunities. Examples of concepts that are built around effective process management include:

- Business Process Re-engineering (BPR);
- Quality Management (including application of ISO 9000 standards);
- Activity-based Management, Costing (ABC), and Budgeting (ABB);

- Process Performance Measurement for Balanced Scorecard (BSC);

- Cycle time improvement.

Processes are the building blocks of organizational activity. They are put in place in order to take inputs, perform activities, and create outputs; in many cases, processes will inter-relate — the output of one feeding the input of another. Some process outputs will be the delivery of a product or service to a client; some may be to other internal users.

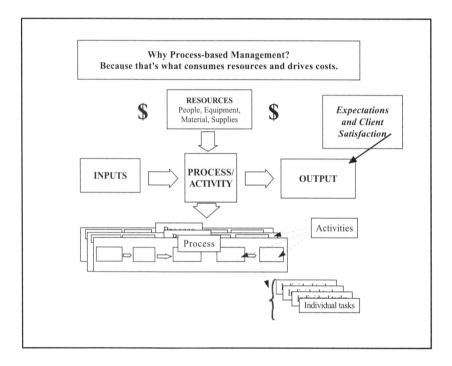

As the picture above shows[1], every process consumes resources, and as a result, effective cost control within any organization is built around effective process management. Processes that are designed and operate effectively consume only the planned or desired levels of resources, whereas processes that do not operate as planned consume excess resources and often become unpredictable in terms of when outputs can be anticipated. The ability of any organization to "do what it promises" depends on consistency between commitments made and capacity to execute.

---

[1] Modified from original ABC slide by FMI Inc. (Focused Management Information).

Controllers must understand process management for at least two critical reasons:

- Cost control has everything to do with eliminating waste and ensuring that processes are designed and managed effectively; and

- The controller manages a number of processes specific to accounting (payables, receivables, payroll, etc.) and these must be managed to minimize cost to the organization.

In addition to cost minimization, effective accounting processes will enhance cash flow. As an example, accurate billings to clients will be collected faster. Effective processes elsewhere in the organization that minimize cycle times will also create significant potential reductions in cash tied up for working capital. Thus a focus on process management is key for every controller.

Process Measurement and Management

In order to move beyond understanding the concepts outlined above, the controller needs facts — measurements that relate to the effectiveness of the activity taking place and the resources being consumed. Traditional cost control, and measuring expenses incurred by responsibility and type of expense, provide little insight into WHERE the resources are being consumed and WHY.

Within the accounting area, and for each of the processes that we will outline in the remainder of this section on resource management, the controller must have facts upon which to manage his or her operations.

Process measurement should include such issues as:

- Cost per transaction;

- Number/percentage of transactions that have to be reprocessed;

- Number of failed transactions;

- Costs incurred in performing non-planned activities within process;

- Volume of transactions;

- Average time per transaction;

- Percentage of transactions completed within the committed time frame.

Effective process definition and measurement also link directly into the concept of defined service standards. Commitments that an organization makes in terms of order turnaround times, response times on telephone calls, and many others are all delivered as the result of a process; thus, service standards are in fact the specifications for design, development, and monitoring of processes.

This handbook cannot cover the whole subject of process management, but today's controllers must research, understand, and apply these concepts in order to provide value-added information about improvement opportunities for management to run the whole enterprise cost effectively as well as being able to run their own accounting area in a way that minimizes costs.

Finally, controllers should always be looking for best practices in terms of process performance; many businesses use these as part of their strategic and business planning. Often referred to as "benchmarking", the organization seeks out those who demonstrate the "best in class" type of performance — especially in areas that are strategically important to the business — and investigates how they can improve their own results towards this objective. Controllers should be able to answer questions about how much an invoice costs to raise or how much a supplier purchase order costs to administer. Knowing this, they can then look at improving their own processes to lower costs and improve process performance.

The Cost of Poor Process Quality

While process management is key to effective use and management of resources, traditional general accounting as well as much cost accounting fails in its efforts to identify and evaluate the financial impact of poor quality on an organization's performance. Most controllers will admit that poor quality or service is costing their organizations money (i.e., either raising costs and depressing profits or just increasing costs in non-profit organizations), but most are unable to identify what these costs actually are.

Controllers who cannot provide management with information about the financial impact of poor quality are failing in their responsibility to protect corporate assets and optimize shareholder equity.

Putting in place processes and systems to track and identify activities that occur because of processes that fail should be a high priority for controllers. Some may already track issues such as scrap costs, rework, warranty, and others, but there is typically much more that could and should be identified. This is a growing issue as the service sector of the economy increases, and traditional costing approaches based on manufacturing-based direct and indirect costing methods are not so easily applied.

The American Society for Quality (ASQ) provides some excellent literature on this concept; there are also publications available through the Institute of Management Accountants (US) on the subject.

Financial Process Management

Typically, the responsibilities of a financial controller will encompass several areas that all designated accountants will have covered as a part of their studies. One of the key advantages of working in an SME is that the financial controller will have the opportunity to apply a broad spectrum of things that he or she has learned and to observe what results ensue.

In this section, we will briefly cover those accounting areas traditionally included in current assets and current liabilities. Specifically, this section will address the management of accounts receivable, accounts payable, and inventory.

Revenues and accounts receivable management

Looking solely at activities that generate cash inflows, transactions are initiated when a sale occurs, which in turn requires generating an invoice as well as recording the transaction and updating the customer's accounts receivable. Subsequently, the business must record the collection of cash and the updating of the accounts receivable due from a customer. In SMEs, it can be a challenge for the organization to be able to perform these functions, and/or to collect the receivable.

Some key accounts receivable management functions that a financial controller must address are:

RESPONSIBILITIES DELEGATED TO STAFF	CORE RESPONSIBILITIES DELEGATED TO THE FINANCIAL CONTROLLER	RESPONSIBILITIES DELEGATED TO A CONSULTANT
• day-to-day administration related to sales, sales invoices, and accounts receivable	• establish procedures and internal control related to the recording of sales, preparation of invoices, collection of revenues, and updating of accounts receivable	
• day-to-day administration related to sales	• establish procedures to record shipping and taxes	
	• establish procedures to maintain the customer database	
	• establish procedures for international sales	

RESPONSIBILITIES DELEGATED TO STAFF	CORE RESPONSIBILITIES DELEGATED TO THE FINANCIAL CONTROLLER	RESPONSIBILITIES DELEGATED TO A CONSULTANT
• day-to-day administration related to the issuing of credit for accounts receivable	• establish policies and procedures covering acceptance of a sale, sales returns, and the issuing of credit	
	• develop reports to support the monitoring of sales and accounts receivable	
• preparation of the summary of sales • preparation of the aging of accounts receivable	• review sales and aged accounts receivable	
• day-to-day administration related to establishing new accounts	• review new accounts	
	• be aware of trends in the industry toward new and/or more cost-effective methods of financing short-term working capital	• discuss with the bank manager or industry associations, benchmark organizations, and others

- Ensure that credit policies and an enforcement process are in place and applied from the moment a proposal or sale occurs.

- Ensure that the process for controlling the provision of goods and services has been tightly linked to a billing process.

- Ensure that any problems with billing are followed up, and that any and all credits and re-billing are reviewed and approved by, at the very least, the controller.

- Establish a monthly reporting format that identifies statistics and plots trends in AR management such as average days outstanding, etc.

- Provide an escalating process for solving problems with accounts receivable — one that ensures that many solutions are considered prior to "cutting off" clients.

- Ensure that processes related to billing and receivables are created and implemented in conjunction with sales, order fulfilment, and other activity centres that are part of the process.

- Determine what risk management considerations apply when the firm is dealing with potential problem accounts such as export accounts, long-term contracts, and others. (Use banks, factors, export insurance, etc.)

- Seek methods to limit the firm's cash exposure on sales/projects involving an extended time period. For example, use milestone billing processes negotiated at the outset of the contract.

- Ensure that pricing policies are established for all goods and services and that there is a process to review and approve any deviations from the standard.

- Ensure that mechanisms and provisions for dealing with things like sales tax exemptions, taxable sales codes, remittance processes, and other mandatory considerations are also in place and compliant with regulations.

The financial controller must work very closely with owners and key managers in the area of AR management. There is a delicate balance to be struck between stimulating sales and increasing the risk of aging accounts receivable. Very often, relationships between the company and its clients and customers are such that ineffective handling of credit issues can create a serious negative impact on relationships.

Controllers must know the business activities so that this process can be planned and managed from the initial quotation to a customer or from their initial order. Many process problems that controllers encounter start with poor information — missing sales tax information, incorrect billing addresses, lack of customers' purchase order numbers, and others. Attention to the front end of this process will often result in significant improvements within the accounting area. Extra costs from activities such as generating credit notes, delays in outstanding collections, incorrect pricing, and many others should be tracked and eliminated through effective process management.

Expenses and Accounts Payable Management

Looking solely at activities that generate cash outflow, transactions are initiated with a purchase of, for example, office supplies, which triggers the receipt of an invoice and the recording of an expense, as well as the updating of the accounts payable due to a supplier. Subsequently, the business must record the payment of cash and the updating of the accounts payable due to the supplier. These functions are a mirror image of functions discussed under "Revenues and accounts receivable management" (page 32).

In conjunction with the cash management functions discussed above, a key area of attention will be the "currency" of amounts due to suppliers. The key to effective cost control as well as cash management in an SME is to control transactions at the source. As was discussed earlier under receivables, control should ideally be exercised before an event is generated. Purchasing, for example, is often not well controlled in an SME, and processes should be reviewed.

The following are some key accounts payable management functions that a financial controller must address.

RESPONSIBILITIES DELEGATED TO STAFF	CORE RESPONSIBILITIES OF THE FINANCIAL CONTROLLER	RESPONSIBILITIES DELEGATED TO A CONSULTANT
• day-to-day administration related to expenses, purchase invoices, and accounts payable	• establish procedures and internal control related to the recording of expenses, the payment of expenses, and the updating of accounts payable	• identify new approaches for payment processing
• day-to-day administration related to expenses	• establish procedures to record shipping and taxes	
	• establish a procedure to maintain a supplier database	
	• establish procedures for international expenditures	
• day-to-day administration related to purchases	• establish policies and procedures related to the authorization of expenditures and purchase on credit	
	• develop reports to support the monitoring of expenses and of accounts payable	

RESPONSIBILITIES DELEGATED TO STAFF	CORE RESPONSIBILITIES OF THE FINANCIAL CONTROLLER	RESPONSIBILITIES DELEGATED TO A CONSULTANT
• preparation of the summary of expenses, including cost of goods sold • preparation of the aging of accounts payable	• review the aging of expenses and accounts payable • review payroll and related disbursements	• prepare payroll • prepare disbursements and related forms for payroll withholdings and employee benefits • prepare payroll summary
• day-to-day administration related to establishing new accounts with suppliers	• review the terms of purchases from suppliers	
	• be aware of trends in the industry towards new and/or more cost-effective methods of financing short-term working capital	• establish annual review of financing structure to ensure optimum framework

- Ensure that there is a process for defining authority to purchase, including limits linked to budgets, strategic plans, and other pre-determined plans.

- Ensure that the process segregates commitments by planned areas such as inventory, capital equipment, and expenses to ensure that the impact on cash flow is assessed at the time of purchase.

- Ensure that all commitments to purchase are documented through requisition slips, purchase orders, and/or equivalent documents.

- Monitor the processes related to approving supplier invoices to make sure that there is adequate control: how easy is it to ascertain that services/goods were provided as required and met the specifications? (Implement and tie in practices like incoming inspections/approvals.)

- Monitor cash flow to the SME's most important suppliers and provide regular (e.g., annual) purchasing power reports on top suppliers. (For example, assess the organization's top 10 or 20 suppliers in terms of dollars spent.) Use these reports as a basis to seek continually improved supply management relationships, including favourable pricing.

- Where appropriate, use the above information to seek supplier "partnerships", ones that look at the overall "distribution channel" costs of obtaining key materials and supplies, and work with supplier partners to reduce the overall costs rather than just the end-user cost to purchase products/services.

- Establish processes to approve miscellaneous expenses such as petty cash, expense account purchases, use of credit cards, etc., so as to ensure adequate review and control.

- Monitor the number of transactions by type of purchase, and seek to reduce overall processing costs on minor items by using corporate purchase agreements, summary billings, blanket orders, credit card orders, etc.

- Structure a process to ensure that all applicable credits from suppliers (including debits for problems identified) are obtained.

- Monitor discounts available from suppliers and seek to balance cash flow management with the receipt of effective payment discounts.

Financial controllers should take an active role in reviewing the company's "purchasing power" — the level of expenditures flowing to key suppliers. In many cases, significant savings can be incurred by consolidating purchases in the hands of fewer suppliers and by re-negotiating terms with those suppliers that are receiving a significant level of business from the company. This used to be true for the acquisition of raw materials but is increasingly applicable to many areas of support costs — transportation, telephone services, and others.

Effective controllers are substantially reducing their process costs and improving timeliness in this area through understanding the nature of their organization's purchasing activity and implementing cost-effective processes focused in key areas. Some examples that controllers should apply would include:

- Use of purchase credit cards for small repetitive items (e.g., office supplies, maintenance supplies);

- Use of summary billing from suppliers where frequent deliveries are summed and submitted on a weekly or monthly basis;

- Focusing certain types of key purchases on a limited number of suppliers to minimize switching and multiple invoicing;

- Use key suppliers as "partners" who manage certain areas of inventory under a kanban-type system and consolidate billings as materials are replenished.

The effective controller will know his or her processing cost in the area of payables and in the profile of transactions. From this, he or she will be able to design processes that drive down costs. Payables is very often an area where significant extra costs are incurred by accounting — by activities such as using "manual cheques" because a supplier was not paid on time; by missed discounts because of processing delays; by receiving multiple invoices from suppliers who cannot meet stock requirements and then ship multiple back orders; or by time spent by clerical staff looking for people to sign invoices from suppliers where there is no name or purchase order. All of these activities cost extra resources and can be opportunities for process improvement.

Payables and receivables — emerging trends

For many organizations payables and/or receivables can involve significant transactional volumes and consume significant resources, making them targets for cost reduction efforts. Effective controllers will firstly understand what makes up their transactional activity in these areas, asking questions such as:

- How many transactions are involved?

- What is the average size/transaction?

- What proportion of transactions are 100% accurately processed?

- Does the "Pareto principle" work here? (i.e., does 80% of the volume account for 20% of the value involved?)

- What does the existing process cost per transaction?

- How fast is the cycle time from start to finish for each transaction?

Using this type of data, many controllers have been developing and applying totally new approaches in order to achieve significant cost reductions. Such changes can include:

- Elimination of credit accounts for small volume buyers and instead accepting credit or debit cards (savings in administrative costs offset fees);

- Simplification of credit approval process for small dollar value buyers;

- Online sales with all purchases by credit card or through third party;

- Use of corporate purchase cards (P-Cards) for all small dollar value transactions (including savings through electronic billing, GL account distribution available from credit card organizations);

- Process automation through the use of EDI (Electronic Data Interchange — computer to computer communication to eliminate paper, improve accuracy, and reduce cycle time);

- Implementation of RDP (Receipt Drive Payment — where buyer or seller no longer use or process an invoice but pay based on contract price and received quantity);

- Implementation of blanket purchase orders, eliminating small purchase quantities on a regular basis with requirements notified computer to computer or by internal requisition;

- Summary billing where regular deliveries are consolidated and billed on a weekly basis.

The effective controller will be constantly seeking ways to reduce transactional costs and enhance cycle times. Rapid changes in technology and the advent of effective and integrated ERP systems are allowing many of these approaches traditionally only available to large organizations to be applied in SMEs.

Inventory Management

Activities related to inventory management generate not only cash inflow but cash outflow as well. When a sale occurs, it will result in a reduction in inventory but will also generate a cash inflow. Acquiring new inventory will result in an increase in inventory while generating a cash outflow.

What inventory management issues the financial controller will be called upon to address will vary depending on whether the business is a manufacturing or a resale concern. Still, whatever the nature of the business, active inventory management can add value to the organization.

Some key inventory management functions that a financial controller must address are:

RESPONSIBILITIES DELEGATED TO STAFF	CORE RESPONSIBILITIES OF THE FINANCIAL CONTROLLER	RESPONSIBILITIES DELEGATED TO A CONSULTANT
• day-to-day administration of inventory	• establish procedures and internal control related to the receipt and shipment of goods from inventory	
	• establish procedures to secure inventory	
• day-to-day recording of transactions	• develop and implement cost-effective IT systems for inventory management	

RESPONSIBILITIES DELEGATED TO STAFF	CORE RESPONSIBILITIES OF THE FINANCIAL CONTROLLER	RESPONSIBILITIES DELEGATED TO A CONSULTANT
	• review and analyze inventory turnover	
	• be aware of trends in the industry towards new and/or more cost-effective methods of inventory management	• have a material management expert review the operation of the organization on a periodic basis

- Link inventory management "approvals to purchase" to payables commitments.

- Ensure that physical controls are established that guarantee that all movements of inventory, such as receiving and issues, create transactions that are registered in the accounting records.

- Carry out a process flow analysis to map physical inventory transactions to book movements, such that paperwork remains linked to physical balances.

- Pay particular attention to controls related to the use of additional materials, and items such as scrapped materials and rework.

- Ensure that the movement of all materials out of the plant is monitored, including that of items such as scrapped materials, and ensure that the company receives the credits due for such sales.

- Review the types of inventory to ensure that physical handling is protecting the items — (e.g., are there special needs in terms of handling, any special storage conditions or temperatures, date coding, etc., required?) — and ensure that stock rotation is being exercised.

- Establish monitoring processes that define at a glance the "content" of the inventory. For example, segregate raw materials from work-in-progress and finished goods, and segregate materials by type (e.g., product or tooling).

- Pay attention to the aging of inventory — ensure that classifications are in place to identify items that are slow-moving or "no-moving". (This is an area of particular importance for distribution organizations, SMEs involved with rapid technological change, etc.)

- Ensure that cash is not being wasted through ineffective inventory management, such as having spare parts on the shelf but buying duplicate parts as required and expensing them.

- Work with suppliers of materials to reduce cash flow by improving performance and reliability — seek improved inventory management as part of key supplier "partnering".

- In multi-location organizations, pay attention to the tendency for inventory to move around with no transaction records appearing under accounting.

- Consider cycle counting for ongoing verification that the book and physical assets are in balance.

- Seek to integrate systems so that materials management transactions — those covering physical inventory — are fully integrated with the financial records.

In many SMEs, the financial controller will be called upon to take an active role in inventory management, not so much as concerns the selection of items, but rather to advise management on the impact of having cash tied up in unproductive inventory and to point out slow-moving, excess, or obsolete items. As an example, while many organizations keep spare maintenance parts in inventory, over 70% of such parts on hand are not required. Either there are more than enough goods stockpiled for safety, or the parts are no longer required or actively used. Financial controllers should have sufficient grounding in inventory management to be able to deal with physical management issues as well as the handling of transactions from a book perspective.

Although inventory is a significant area of investment in many SMEs, scant resources may be available for materials management. As such, the financial controller should watch inventories closely and be able to advise management not only on the financial implications of given scenarios but also on the business aspects which they trigger. For example, ensure that coordination is taking place between sales-on-demand, production, and quantity planning, and that customer service levels are being tracked to determine what inventory levels to maintain.

Inventory and lean management practices

Controllers will welcome the operational focus on lean management. This concept, pioneered by Toyota and adopted by many others, focuses on the elimination of all areas of organizational waste. One key result of waste is the need to carry excessive inventory. Controllers should work closely with operational management to define the need for any level of inventory at all and strive to develop operational processes and vendor relationships that minimize or eliminate such investments. This can be achieved in manufacturing by moving from a "push" process, where output is created in anticipation of demand, to a "pull" process, where production only occurs in response to specific customer demand. To achieve this and still meet client expectations for rapid delivery, operational processes must be streamlined to minimize cycle times and increase flexibility. Such approaches can bring significant benefits but will also demand significant changes in areas such as shop-floor organization and reporting, planning, scheduling, accountability, vendor relationships, costing approaches, and many others.

The concept can also work in many other industries such as retailing, distribution, and others, through progressive approaches to supply-chain management. While detailed discussion of these topics is outside the scope of this book, controllers should research and be aware of emerging trends in these areas.

Payroll and Benefits

Payroll, source deductions, and the administration of employee benefits is often a core process for controllers. While in the past many smaller organizations subcontracted their payroll, the advent of integrated software for small business that is supported with frequent and up-to-date payroll modules has made it possible to carry out this work in house cost effectively.

Whatever portion of the payroll process the controller decides to perform internally, it will involve some level of resource. Some of the key issues that the controller must address are included in the following chart. (Note that, in some cases, these functions will be handled by a Human Resources individual if one is on staff.)

RESPONSIBILITIES DELEGATED TO STAFF	CORE RESPONSIBILITIES OF THE FINANCIAL CONTROLLER	RESPONSIBILITIES DELEGATED TO A CONSULTANT
• day-to-day data collection • account reconciliations of pay and benefits • generation of routine pay or • work with outside payroll organization • reconcile payroll bank account if used	• set policy on use of outside v. inside payroll • handle management pay (depending upon owners) • work with owner to establish compensation framework • work with owners to define retention strategy for key staff • work with owners and consultants to develop annual merit and other increases • establish the pay system	• define legislation that may be applicable (annual review) • support to establish set of competitive pay rates • advise on benefit plans and structure and periodic review of carriers • advise on structuring of taxable v. non-taxable benefits

RESPONSIBILITIES DELEGATED TO STAFF	CORE RESPONSIBILITIES OF THE FINANCIAL CONTROLLER	RESPONSIBILITIES DELEGATED TO A CONSULTANT
	• check monthly summaries of pay clearing and remittances • review additions to payroll and changes to pay rates	• support in defining hiring criteria
	• develop policies for issues such as contractor v. employee	

• Work with owners to ensure that issues such as pay confidentiality for certain members of staff are handled either by separate "executive" payroll or other approaches.

• Create a set of pay rates and a progression framework so that people will be hired at the correct level and can obtain increases as their skills improve.

• In cases where there are discrepancies between "market" rates for positions and the "standard", work with the owners to define how a progressive approach to adjustment can be made.

• Establish criteria for approaches to pay "adders" such as overtime rates, call-in allowances, premiums for shifts, and other items.

• Establish criteria for types of employment to ensure guidelines are in place for dealing with issues such as temporary staff, part-time workers, contract staff, and others. Additionally, controllers should carefully review the classifications between "employee" and "contractor" or "consultant", especially where individuals who are not employees are spending all or most of their time working for the controller's organization. This situation can give rise to a reclassification by Canada Revenue Agency (CRA), resulting in the employer becoming liable for 100% of both employer and employee premiums for employment insurance (EI) and Canada Pension Plan (CPP). It is recommended that controllers review CRA Interpretation Bulletin RC4110 dealing with employee or contractor relationships. Creation of a company-specific checklist to assess individuals might be an effective tool to assist in identifying situations where this relationship might be questionable.

• Create and communicate policies in areas such as pay dates (when overtime pay will be included in pay calculations and key input dates), to ensure those feeding data to accounting are aware of their responsibility for data input.

- Establish policies in key areas such as use of company cars, personal use, and mileage allowances so that it is clear as to what the taxation impacts are, and what responsibility the company and the employee take given positions on taxable benefits and declarations of income.

- Continually review benefit plans and framework to ensure that the approach offered is consistent with market "best practice" to attract and retain staff (e.g., look at "cafeteria approach" with some degree of flexibility).

- Create specific timetables for pay dates, benefit remittance dates, and source deduction dates to ensure that people on staff make remittances in a timely manner.

- Establish effective controls for changes to any aspects of payroll — staff additions, pay rate changes, or gross pay levels.

A controller in an SME will often be faced with a framework for pay and benefits that has evolved over time as the business has grown from infancy to a level of maturity. Implementing policy and standards for this is sometimes a major challenge for the controller in working with the owner who carries a lot of history, which will drive the desire for many exceptions. Failure to deal with this issue will create larger problems as inequities within the system of compensation are identified and spread. In addition, there is the temptation to establish arrangements for compensation that avoid taxes.

This can create ethical issues for controllers, as they must firmly establish their position for correct treatment of compensation that is compliant with legislation and, in so doing, create barriers for what owners may want to do. The best way to deal with this is to try to find alternative approaches that are compliant yet provide the required incentives for employees and others, and bring in expert advice which will be able to both support the position as well as suggest other approaches.

Recognition and Rewards

In addition to routine areas of pay and benefits there are certain other approaches to recognition and rewards for staff that can lead to taxable treatment. These vary and are constantly being influenced by rulings from tax authorities. Controllers should remain aware of these issues to ensure that the most effective approaches are adopted. These may include issues such as:

- paid memberships in business and social activities;
- use of company property or facilities;

- meals and meal allowances;

- gifts for employees;

- cash awards for employees;

- use of travel benefits by employees on personal travel;

- attendance at conferences and workshops in vacation areas;

- parking spaces provided by employer (paid for by employer).

The use of a tax advisor is **strongly recommended** as controllers may not have adequate time available to stay on top of changes and be aware of the many alternatives. Subscription to tax advisory services, which usually identify key decisions, can be another advantage, but in many cases the various options may not be clear, as every organization has unique situations.

While monetary and non-monetary awards create issues for the controller to deal with, it is important that, as a member of the management team, the controller always be looking for ways to assist in the motivation of staff and the building of morale.

Cash Management

Cash management functions are limited to those transactions that directly involve the bank (some may overlap functions that are considered under planning management), as well as the effective management of working capital (processes related to receivables, payables, and inventory) and balance sheet management (timing and approach to capital purchases).

Often, both short- and long-term bank loans will have been secured on company assets or even on privately owned assets of the key owners or shareholders. Financial controllers must scrutinize the lending agreements to understand and then monitor any loan criteria and covenants that apply. One of the key areas that lending institutions monitor is the organization's ability to manage within its anticipated levels of required funding without contravening its bank loan agreements.

The following are some key cash management functions that a financial controller must address:

RESPONSIBILITIES DELEGATED TO STAFF	CORE RESPONSIBILITIES OF THE FINANCIAL CONTROLLER	RESPONSIBILITIES DELEGATED TO A CONSULTANT
	• develop procedures and internal control for cash and petty cash • develop procedures and internal control for short-term investments and short-term debt	
• prepare periodic bank reconciliations	• monitor and maintain the cash position • compare the current cash flow to the forecast • compare current financial ratios to loan criteria established by the banks	
• prepare deposits, cash receipts	• review deposits	
• prepare cheques • prepare cheque disbursement summary	• authorize cheque disbursements • review cheque disbursement summary	
	• review all cash advances	
	• review all payments and advances to shareholders • review payments to shareholders and ensure that they are within the terms of the bank loan agreements	
	• organize the capital structure to both maximize interest income and minimize interest expense • co-ordinate financial transactions to minimize bank service charges	• review with the bank manager

RESPONSIBILITIES DELEGATED TO STAFF	CORE RESPONSIBILITIES OF THE FINANCIAL CONTROLLER	RESPONSIBILITIES DELEGATED TO A CONSULTANT
	• co-ordinate policies and procedures used in revenue and AR management, expense and AP management, and inventory management with respect to optimizing cash flows	
	• forecast short and long-term cash flows • update the bank on the company's current operations and future requirements • secure commitment for short and long-term debt to support forecasts	• verify with the bank manager as to how reasonable your cash flow figures are and the underlying estimates you have made concerning interest rates, the rate of inflation, currency fluctuations, cost of living, and other such variables
	• stay aware of trends in industry regarding new and/or more effective methods to improve the cash inflow and outflow cycle	

Short-term cash management should be a top priority for financial controllers. Regular monitoring of bank balances, as well as the preparation and review of daily, weekly and monthly cash plans, and forecasts is a routine measure that should be in place. Disbursements through cash, cheques, bank transfers, and all other methods must be strictly controlled.

Financial controllers realize very quickly that in owner-operated businesses, decisions that have a significant impact on cash flows are often made with a limited degree of consultation. The only way to deal with this reality is to develop a close working relationship with the owner so that communications are at their best — not to stop this type of event from occurring but to be aware of their possibility and to limit surprises.

Some examples of practical approaches to effective cash management include:

- Establish realistic expectations for financing needs, taking into consideration things such as the ability/desirability of making interest payments and servicing debt.

- Continually monitor the existing uses of cash through cash forecasts and short-term loans/investments, receivables management, and supplier payment management.

- Be vigilant concerning the organization's financing structure and all covenants that may exist.

- Be aware of alternative methods and sources of short- and long-term financing.

- Maintain ongoing communication with lenders and investors concerning the company's financing requirements.

Cash management is probably THE most important role for a controller in most enterprises; cash is the life-blood of the organization and many smaller enterprises fail not because the business case is poor but because they run out of cash and fail to manage this limited resource effectively. The controller must ensure that an effective forecasting system is in place and that cash is monitored on a consistent basis.

Costing, Profit Management, and Management Accounting Methods

A controller's greatest value comes from helping the owners and other managers make decisions that lead to the achievement of business plans. While ensuring that the day-to-day accounting is performed adequately and at minimum cost is important, it will not differentiate the average controller from the more effective one.

In order to add value in the management accounting area, the controller must first learn the business he or she is working for, and how it operates in terms of relating to clients and customers and applying its resources in ways that lead to success. The more the controller becomes engaged in the planning processes, the greater will be the understanding of the "key success factors" of the organization. These will vary by organization but in most cases the following areas will be important:

- Having a "cost map" for the organization that identifies where the major pools of costs are assigned in order to set control priorities (i.e., a high-level view of how the costs build up to the total cost base);

- Ensuring that a process is in place for the responsible accounting of all expenditures (i.e., ownership for the costs incurred through some basic type of departmental cost structure within the GL);

- Target or objective costs for products and services that are being produced and provided to clients (either product or process standard costs, preferably using ABC techniques);

- Cost collection methods that allow actual costs of products and services to be developed and compared to target costs (whether the organization is product or service based) such as:

  ➢ Effective controls of materials issues and usage,

  ➢ Effective labour cost controls and assignments to products and/or services either through cost pools or time sheets,

  ➢ Production control tracking that identifies equipment utilization for products created,

  ➢ Assignment of indirect costs to specific products or services;

- Process for planning future product or service initiatives that establish resources required, and incremental costs of production and delivery using processes such as modelling and simulation;

- Financial tracking of the utilization of the fixed asset base (manufacturing assets) to identify idle capacity and alternative uses, as well as "down time" and other process problems.

The ability to carry out effective analytical work and costing will depend on three critical issues:

- The desire for and understanding of this information by owners/ managers;

- The resources available to the controller to do this work; and

- The way in which the controller assigns limited time.

Dealing with the understanding of managers is an ongoing job for the controller, consistent with building effective interpersonal relationships. This and the other two factors demand that controllers use a high degree of focus on where they apply their attention. Controllers making the transition from a larger organization to a small one will have to scale back their expectations of what can be achieved given the limited resources. This is a key area where controllers should "step back" from their financial role and ask the question "what would I need to know if I were to run this organization with an eye to profitability"? It is this perspective that the controller starts with in becoming of value to the owners and other managers, and this, in turn, begins with getting to know the business and how it operates.

Facilities Management

Most financial controllers will inherit a number of responsibilities related to facilities management. Considered one by one, such functions may not seem that important, but ignoring them will reduce the organization's effectiveness. If the financial controller is to add value in the area of facilities management, it is important that routine activities be delegated, and that consultants be engaged to address complex issues.

Some key facilities management functions that a financial controller must address are:

RESPONSIBILITIES DELEGATED TO STAFF	CORE RESPONSIBILITIES OF THE FINANCIAL CONTROLLER	RESPONSIBILITIES DELEGATED TO A CONSULTANT
• day-to-day administration	• plan for adequate resources and include them in the operational budget	• recommendations on complex issues
	• establish policies such as spending authorization and implement internal control	
	• participate in all negotiations related to facilities management	

The Facilities Management Checklist (see Exhibit 3-C in the Appendix) can be used as a resource for managing the buildings and land, plant equipment, office and computer equipment, office services, and company vehicles of an SME.

Project-Related Financial Management

On occasion, there may be opportunities for the financial controller to participate in one-off projects. The financial controller in response to stakeholders' concerns may initiate some of these projects. For example, as a result of customers complaining about shoddy goods, the financial controller could launch a program to increase quality control using a team approach.

The financial controller will be able to add value if he or she is up to date on management accounting methods. Depending on the complexity of the issue at hand, it may be necessary to seek the advice of consultants.

The following list provides ideas on some specific areas for project-related cost improvement studies:

- Look at the organization as a collection of multiple "processes" and seek ways to perform them cost effectively.

- Quality management, applied effectively, can reduce waste in any organization: make a point to investigate where waste is occurring, as traditional reporting may not identify this weakness.

- Obtain feedback from key stakeholders on the effectiveness of current processes and procedures; this would include clients and employees, who may have a very definite insight as to where improvements are possible.

- Ensure that business systems are helping the organization to reduce costs and improve the flow of information. Systems based on the concept of "enterprise resource planning" and integrated systems that use a "single database" approach can provide assistance in this area.

- Ensure that communications into and out of the organization are performed cost effectively. The field of telecommunications is changing rapidly, so keep abreast of developments to be able to reduce costs and improve services on a continual basis.

- As much as possible, replace paper processes with technology. For example, move data entry to the source by providing sales staff with laptop computers.

- Monitor support systems, such as fax machines, e-mail, photocopiers, etc., to ensure that technology is being applied cost effectively.

- Monitor the impact of technology on customers: advanced automation may reduce costs, but it can also significantly reduce client satisfaction.

- Consider areas such as security and privacy. With electronic commerce, security of access becomes more critical, and adequate controls must be in place.

- Recognize that training and upgrading staff is critical, and ensure that training expenditures are well planned and congruent with the future needs of the business rather than just meeting the criterion of "so many hours per year".

The controller in an SME has to be aware of the host of changes taking place in, around, and outside of the organization, which is a somewhat daunting task. The key to handling it successfully is the ability to scan developments and then initiate investigation or action when and as required, while still working within the time constraints discussed in Chapter 1. Judicious selection and use of external consultants may support this process.

To ensure an adequate return on investment in this area, the financial controller should consider selecting consultant "partners" in critical areas, in order to minimize the "learning curve" required before they can add value to the organization.

Other tasks as assigned

Most controllers face a host of administrative tasks in addition to the facilities issues outlined above. These can be incredibly time wasting for the controller, and time spent on these issues will take away some capacity to work in other areas. Controllers should take action to minimize the impact of these activities. Suggestions for improvement include:

- Identify all non-core tasks on a checklist and assign/delegate wherever possible (this can include delegating to non-accounting staff).

- For areas that include "problem solving" such as courier companies, security issues, cleaning, maintenance, office equipment repair and maintenance — identify by list the person to contact and services provided. Make this available to all staff so that they can solve problems themselves (e.g., post on an Intranet site or put a memo in "Outlook" or an equivalent program).

- Minimize the need for intervention in key areas — put partner agreements in place and/or use credit card purchasing with organizations for services such as providing office supplies.

- Learn to say "No" — some types of problems just have to be pushed back to the individual. While the controller wants to be supportive and a problem solver, individuals in organizations must exercise personal accountability.

- Be wary of tasks delegated by owners that seem to be outside the scope of the job — be prepared to discuss concerns about these if they become common, and be prepared to suggest alternative ways of dealing with the issues.

- Use outside advisors where practical; often, controllers will be asked for financial, HR, or legal advice. Avoid the trap of becoming an internal unpaid consultant; there are opportunities to put arrangements in place with local specialists who can offer these services and others to all employees (may also include areas such as retirement planning).

This aspect of the controller's role relates directly back to the discussion on time management in Chapter 1. Controllers in many organizations become THE persons who handle all administrative roles, and should constantly look at their qualifications and experience and ask whether the organization is obtaining the best value by having the controller carry out these tasks.

Chapter 4

Relationship Management: Building the Networks for Success

Summary ☞

Effective controllers work as part of an organization's management team, contributing knowledge and working closely with other managers. To do this they need to spend adequate time on building both internal and external relationships. This chapter starts with understanding the needs of owners, business leaders, and other key managers. Additionally, the controller needs to understand his or her own personal leadership style and build solid relationships with staff as well as external "partners". An effective controller creates a network of advisors who can be called upon to provide specialist advice in those areas to which he or she cannot commit the necessary time to remain fully up to date.

In most (if not all) organizations, people are the most valuable resource, but their value is often overlooked. The financial controller can add value to the organization if he or she is able to effectively manage its human resources and relationships.

PEOPLE AND RELATIONSHIP MANAGEMENT	HOURS PER YEAR	ASSIGNMENT OF RESPONSIBILITY
Internal relationships: Owners/Managers	80	• the controller has a clear understanding of the needs of the owner
Internal relationships: Staff	265	• the controller implements procedures that address the management of staff
Internal relationships: Self-management	40	• the controller implements an ongoing program to maintain and upgrade his or her individual competencies
External relationships	80	• The controller implements a program to maintain external relationships

Internal Relationships: Owners/Managers

One of the critical functions that the financial controller must manage is internal relationships with the owner. He or she will be perceived to add value when viewed by the owner as both a confidante and a valuable business resource.

The following are some key internal relationship functions that a financial controller must address.

RESPONSIBILITIES DELEGATED TO STAFF	CORE RESPONSIBILITIES OF THE FINANCIAL CONTROLLER	RESPONSIBILITIES DELEGATED TO A CONSULTANT
	• understand the structure of the organization	
	• understand the needs of the owner	• use a consultant for specialized or complex issues
	• identify individual strengths and weaknesses	

Structure of the organization

The new financial controller must clearly understand the ownership and management structure of the organization. In most cases, the financial controller of an SME is also the senior financial manager in the organization. He or she will be required to handle a broad range of responsibilities. However, what those specific responsibilities are will be determined by the structure of the organization. Typical organizational structures could include the financial controller reporting directly to:

- the owner who is active as president, CEO, or equivalent;

- one of the owners holding the above title, with other owners (or family members) being active in the business;

- one of the owners as above, but where all other owners are "silent partners" in the business;

- a general manager, president, CEO, or other senior manager who works for one or more owners of a privately held company;

- the president, CEO, or general manager of a publicly held company.

It is important to understand what this relationship is so that the financial controller can "frame" financial advice to correspond with the given structure.

Needs of the owner

Financial controllers in SMEs generally find themselves faced with a much broader range of duties than they would in a larger organization where many of the individual tasks will have been delegated to specialized staff. This is further complicated in the case of owner-managed organizations, where the principals often have a strong personal financial involvement.

Fulfilling the needs of the owner may require that the financial controller:

- keep all day-to-day administrative aspects of the business running smoothly;

- take full responsibility for all financial matters, including

  ➢ managing the processing of all financial transactions,

  ➢ managing cash on a day-to-day basis,

  ➢ managing data processing and information systems;

- be aware of the options that owners/managers have to extract remuneration and profits from their business and give advice on the implications of adopting one option over another;

- anticipate the impact of business decisions on the owner's personal finances;

- foresee the financial repercussions of the owner's business decisions on the organization (owners often make decisions without giving enough consideration to such aspects);

- keep the owner aware of problems that may arise in other areas of the business;

- manage relationships with external bodies, including trouble-shooting when problems arise;

- ensure the organization is compliant with all applicable legislation, including health and safety provisions, regulations affecting hours of work, labour codes, etc.

The following are some of the factors that the financial controller of an SME may have to ascertain and make allowances for:

- To ascertain impacts, the controller must understand the owner's personal financial situation in addition to the business position in areas such as tax planning, security for loans and debts, relationships with customers and/or suppliers, etc.

- Commitments may exist contractually between active owners and other investors governing profit-sharing agreements, shareholder agreements, levels of authority in decision-making, etc.

- Personal relationships may influence communications and decision-making (e.g., the level of information shared outside business hours, trade-off agreements between family members to recognize their areas of personal expertise or interests, etc.).

- There may be areas of conflict, including disagreements between the active owners and other parties, as well as conflicts involving owners, family members, and other private shareholders, past or present.

The new financial controller must be very sensitive to the human dynamics at play in the SME, especially if it is privately owned and closely held. Owners typically keep certain information private for fear of it becoming widely known, and will become less guarded, even towards the financial controller, only inasmuch as they begin to recognize that person's integrity. Instilling trust in the owners will take time and should be recognized as a cumulative process that starts on the first day of work. In summary, to be fully effective in the organization, a financial controller will require strong human relations skills.

Personal strengths and weaknesses

To be effective, the financial controller must accumulate a certain body of knowledge, skills, and practical experience. Given the scope of issues that he or she must face and the fact that the business world is rapidly changing, it is imperative that the financial controller not only maintain basic competencies, but also strive to upgrade them on an on-going basis.

If controllers as individuals are able to assess their current competencies and identify the competencies that would make them more effective financial controllers, they should be able to develop an action plan that will allow them to do so and add value to the organization.

Some of the critical skills and abilities that the financial controller of an SME should possess are:

- looking at the financials from a business perspective (thinking like an owner);

- continually thinking ahead (e.g., developing contingency plans based on "what if" scenarios);

- relating well at all levels — from board members and senior management to junior clerks;

- being able to communicate financial data in non-accounting terms to a broad set of users;

- knowing how to organize and delegate routine accounting tasks, freeing up time to concentrate on higher management functions;

- grasping the "big picture" (e.g., potential impacts on owners, ethical considerations, long-term external relationships, etc.);

- anticipating the requirements of others (e.g., owners, managers, staff);

- being action-oriented — showing leadership in addressing issues as they arise;

- knowing where to obtain support resources in specialist areas when these are required;

- "leading by example" — the financial controller is the one most often in the office.

Internal Relationships: Staff

In many organizations, the responsibility for payroll is assigned to the financial controller. In connection with payroll, controllers often inherit responsibilities associated with the management of staff, to which time is allocated only if an emergency arises.

If you review the number of hours that a financial controller can expect to allocate to activities involving staff relationships, it is clear that this is a critical function. By developing a clear understanding of the responsibilities that effective internal relationships entail, the financial controller should be in a position to add value to the organization.

The following are some key staff relationship functions that a financial controller must address.

RESPONSIBILITIES DELEGATED TO STAFF	CORE RESPONSIBILITIES OF THE FINANCIAL CONTROLLER	RESPONSIBILITIES DELEGATED TO A CONSULTANT
	• obtain agreement on key HR policies	
	• implement a human resource management program	• contract with an HRM expert
• ability to self-assess	• evaluate and monitor administration of the accounting department	• support with coaching and training
	• train other managers	

Key success factors for effective HR management

The most valuable resource for any organization is its people. They are the driving force behind innovation, creativity, effective supplier relationships, and effective client relationships. In fact, people create an organization's competitive advantage. Controllers should ensure that within their own organization (and across the organization if they have overall HR management) that the following key factors are addressed within an HR management system:

• communications to and from staff,

• education and training of staff, and

• monitoring of staff satisfaction.

Staff are involved in the day-to-day activities of any organization and their continual input can provide valuable insight into improvement opportunities. This culture starts at the top of any organization and sets the tone for all subsequent employee engagement. Every employee must have a clear understanding of where the organization is going and how he or she fits in. In addition, employees must know the "rules of the game" through clear HR policies and procedures.

Education and training is also critical. Staff must be encouraged to continue to grow in their skills in ways that can help them develop personally as well as become more effective within the organization. Education forms the key basis of understanding the reality of an organization's mission and the challenges that it faces in achieving its goals. Education allows employees to see their own role in the context of the overall organization. Training provides support to employees through helping them develop the new skills and knowledge necessary to grow their personal careers and their value to the organization. Controllers must ensure that there is a structured approach to training that clearly links personal growth with performance expectations. They must also ensure that education and training receive adequate funding relative to their importance.

Finally, controllers must ensure a feedback system is in place that allows management to assess the levels of employee satisfaction. From this, key issues can be identified and addressed. Continued and regular surveys of employee satisfaction should be undertaken, and trends tracked and monitored.

Implement a human resource management program

Although day-to-day human resource management is the responsibility of every manager and every supervisor, financial controllers in larger organizations can assume that this area of responsibility is backed up with established structures, policies, and procedures. Such measures ensure that hiring, training in job responsibilities, pay arrangements, and even performance measurement and termination are conducted on a fair and equitable basis, and that corporate practices comply with applicable statutes and legislation.

In the SME environment, it often comes as a surprise to the financial controller to find out that these issues have sometimes not been addressed systematically. People have been hired and compensated on a "case-by-case" basis, without comparing remuneration to the going market rate or even to the pay provisions governing other positions in the organization. Overtime pay might have been negotiated on an individual basis. Managers may even have done things that are clearly in contravention of work-related legislation.

The impact of SMEs not establishing formal human resource management policies and procedures often surfaces only later. Staff motivation declines, key personnel are lured away from the company by better offers, key goals of the organization are not achieved. In addition, the company may become embroiled in legal disputes because of things such as unsafe working conditions, wrongful dismissal, or even discrimination in hiring and work practices.

The first step in implementing a comprehensive human resource management program is to devise a framework that will guide the development of appropriate HR policies and procedures.

Devise a framework for human resource management

One way to formulate a human resource management framework is to think through the life cycle of employees. Once recruited and hired by the organization, they are trained and coached, gain skills and experience, are promoted, and may eventually leave.

Aside from managing the employee cycle, the organization must also remember to comply with a host of regulations. Bearing all this in mind, an effective human resource management framework will:

- determine the process for hiring employees —

  - ➢ establish formal hiring policies that will address issues such as fairness, and use them as a guide to devise and implement specific procedures,

  - ➢ establish procedures for recruitment and interviewing,

  - ➢ establish procedures for approving new hires,

  - ➢ establish an orientation program,

  - ➢ at all stages, provide a clear description of the required competencies and responsibilities;

- create an infrastructure for training, development, and promotion —

  - ➢ establish a process to clarify expectations concerning key responsibilities,

  - ➢ establish a formal process of performance evaluation,

  - ➢ create an objective compensation system that is based on performance,

  - ➢ provide a program of ongoing training;

- create a process to address discipline, termination, and workforce reduction —

  - ➢ establish formal discipline and termination processes that adhere to all laws and regulations,

  - ➢ establish plans to address planned and unplanned workforce reductions.

Be aware of legislation and regulations that govern human resource management

A host of laws and regulations govern human resource management. Examples are listed in the following table.

AREAS OF LEGISLATION	COMMENTS AND FURTHER ACTION

Federal legislation
 	
• Income tax (and liabilities to pay)
• *Canada Pension Plan* (except Quebec)
• Employment Insurance
• Canada Human Rights legislation
• Right to vote under the *Elections Act*
• Some areas of Family Law
• *Canada Labour Code* (where federally incorporated)
	• Most labour legislation is the responsibility of the provincial government; however, some key federal areas to address include:
	  ➤ Income Tax, EI, and CPP
	  ➤ Federal Human Rights legislation and Family Law (possible impact)
	  ➤ Application of *Canada Labour Code*

Provincial legislation • Human Rights codes • Provincial Income Tax • Employment Standards legislation • Minimum Wage legislation • Pension Plan legislation • Health and Safety (including WHMIS areas) • Workers' Compensation legislation • Health Care plans and criteria • Labour Relations acts • Pay and Employment Equity • Provincial areas of Family Law	• Provincial law is probably the greatest area of concern for most SMEs. Key aspects are those related to Employment Standards legislation, such as hours of work, overtime wage criteria, minimum wage rates, vacation pay, notice and termination requirements, etc., as well as situations which require the granting of time off, such as maternity leave • Financial controllers should be aware of applicable legislation and make sure that the company's policies, procedures, and manual are in compliance
Municipal legislation • Numerous bylaws • Some election legislation	• Not "high profile", but covers areas like planning, building codes, use of premises, licensing, smoking, etc.

Provide management of the accounting department

Managing the accounting department can be viewed as a process that consists of the following steps:

- identify all functions performed by the accounting department;

- identify and secure the resources required to perform these functions;

- implement a program to identify potential bottlenecks and monitor performance on a continual basis.

Identify all functions performed by the accounting department

In the process of identifying the functions performed by the accounting department, the financial controller should also gather information about things like the skills and competencies required to conduct relevant activities, the average number of transactions per period, and the time frame in which they generally occur.

One way for the financial controller to add value in this area could be to question the value of every function that is performed. Could some be simplified or eliminated? Is it possible to take advantage of the value chain and transfer certain functions to suppliers or customers? The following table provides guidance on the types of information that could be collected.

Accounting Functions

Area of Work	Type of Data Required	Results
Purchasing and payables	• number of suppliers • number of purchase orders per week • number of receipts per week • number of line items per receipt • number of invoices received per week • number of cheques issued per week • number of account reconciliations • other reconciliations • number of remittances (tax, etc.)	

Area of Work	Type of Data Required	Results
	• time spent on problem accounts • nature of reports being created • time spent on reports • time spent on other activities • aged trial balance of payables due	
Billing and receivables	• number of customers • number of billings per month • number of receipts per month • average number of receipts per day • number of credits issued per month • time spent on overdue recovery • time spent on resolving problems • time spent on tax remittances • trends in days' sales outstanding • aged trial balance overdue	
Payroll processing	• number of employees • types and methods of employees' pay • number of tax jurisdictions • benefit programs in place • time spent on benefit claims • number of remittances to carriers • time spent to reconcile and pay benefits to carriers • time spent on input processing	

AREA OF WORK	TYPE OF DATA REQUIRED	RESULTS
Inventory management	• number of inventory items • turnover rate/days' cost of sales • write-down policies • risk/review for obsolescence • number of issues per month • number of receipts per month (see AP) • number of returns/adjustments per month • history of count variances	
Fixed asset management	• number of additions per month • time spent on analysis	
Cash and bank management	• number of deposits per week • number of items per deposit • other types of processing • time spent on bank reconciliation	
Costing activity	• number of pieces of data collected (labour, material, etc.) • time spent on creating cost data • time spent on data entry • time spent on report generation • number of reports distributed • review/proof/validation of costing data (by comparison to estimates, etc.)	

Identify and secure the resources required to perform all functions

In identifying the resources required to perform accounting department functions, the financial controller must take into account a number of factors, such as:

- possibility of delegating responsibility to other staff;
- segregation of duties and confidentiality of information (payroll);
- back-up for holidays, sick leave, and loss of staff;
- ongoing training;
- forecasted growth of existing or new operations;
- adoption of new processes or information technology;
- constraints imposed by union contracts.

In securing the resources necessary to perform all the functions that take place in the accounting department, the financial controller must consider issues such as:

- competencies of existing staff;
- cost benefits of outsourcing activities;
- plans of the other departments within the organization.

Delegation, accountability and cross-training

Effective controllers will ensure that processes have been well designed, clearly documented, and staff trained in their execution. It will be important to bring together a schedule that identifies the work to be done, when it is due, who is responsible (and who is the back-up person) and how the work should be performed. A chart such as that shown in Appendix II, Exhibit 4-A can be useful and, if circulated within the organization, can also help controllers avoid many of the day-to-day questions about reports and accounting processes by defining a "go to" person for each key activity.

Implement a program to identify potential bottlenecks and monitor performance on an ongoing basis

The financial controller must develop a process that will objectively monitor the performance of the department. For example:

- for each critical accounting function, identify benchmarks that would give advance warning of bottlenecks developing (such as delays in closing the monthly general ledger and continued requests for overtime);
- elicit comments via a suggestion box;
- monitor overtime or requests for temporary assistance.

Internal Relationships: Self-management

Self-management means different things to different people. In this document, it is defined as the ability to understand and manage one's personal beliefs and behaviours in ways that create and support identified or desired objectives. Self-management embraces the following competencies:

- understanding personal dynamics, including recognizing one's emotions and knowing one's own strengths and weaknesses;

- self-control;

- self-confidence;

- taking responsibility for one's personal behaviour;

- time management;

- stress management;

- career planning.

The following are some key self-management functions that a financial controller must address.

RESPONSIBILITIES DELEGATED TO STAFF	CORE RESPONSIBILITIES OF THE FINANCIAL CONTROLLER	RESPONSIBILITIES DELEGATED TO A CONSULTANT
	• identify and assess one's competencies	• in conjunction with a peer, review competencies
	• design a program to develop appropriate competencies	
	• integrate self-management functions with normal routine	
	• identify and assess personal priorities in relation to career	

Identify and assess competencies in the area of self-management

The first step for the financial controller to complete in the area of self-management is to identify and assess his or her current competencies. To gain some perspective and increase the chances of an objective assessment, it may be useful to seek feedback from a peer.

Design a program to develop appropriate competencies

An efficient and effective financial controller will be very proficient at self-management. He or she will demonstrate a consistent ability to grow in all areas of personal effectiveness, consistently use sophisticated self-management strategies, act as a role model for others with respect to understanding and using self-knowledge to increase professional effectiveness, and integrate personal values with personal and business effectiveness in a wide range of business situations.

After the individual has completed an assessment of his or her competencies and compared these abilities with the performance level expected of an experienced financial controller, he or she can design a program to bring all of his or her self-management skills to the same high standard.

Integrate self-management activities into one's normal routine

To become more efficient and effective, the financial controller should strive consciously to incorporate self-management skills and practices into his or her normal routine. Devoting some time to more obvious functions such as time management, stress management, and career planning is relatively straight-forward. Integrating subjective activities into the normal routine, such as recognizing one's emotions and understanding personal dynamics, is much more difficult, and these activities are in fact very easy to overlook. Still, when the financial controller makes the effort to implement self-management techniques and activities, his or her effectiveness and efficiency will increase, which in turn adds value to the organization.

Identify and assess personal priorities in relation to one's career

Traditional thinking has evolved, and we now recognize that "the whole person comes to work". The idea that one can segregate one's personal life from life at work is just not realistic. Every one of us is a unique individual who lives in his or her own world yet shares this space with many others.

As a financial controller, in addition to having to deal with your own personal life, you often inherit the role of father or mother figure to the organization: you may find yourself mentoring the owner and even parenting the staff. For some financial controllers, work eventually seems to consume all waking and even sleeping hours. If the feeling develops that you "have no life outside of work", this is a bad situation, both from the organization's perspective and from the individual's. Productivity declines and morale drops, so in spite of the temptation to just keep working until everything that needs doing gets done, a serious effort must be made to balance work and private time. This is not an easy task, and every financial controller must realize that he or she alone can set priorities in life and take charge of the situation.

As a starting point, the financial controller should take some time to prepare his or her individual vision and mission statements, and this formal set of statements should not be limited to the financial controller's career: it should encompass his or her entire life so that the individual will then be able to balance work and leisure time.

Internal Relationships: Leadership

Most would agree that the ability to demonstrate leadership skills is a critical competency for successful financial controllers to possess; however, leadership is a concept that means different things to different people. Some of the components of leadership that will be discussed include strategic thinking and communication, coaching and team-building, and corporate values such as integrity.

The following are some key leadership functions that a financial controller must address.

RESPONSIBILITIES DELEGATED TO STAFF	CORE RESPONSIBILITIES OF THE FINANCIAL CONTROLLER	RESPONSIBILITIES DELEGATED TO A CONSULTANT
	• understand the vision and mission of the owner	
• understanding the vision and mission of the financial controller	• formulate a vision and mission for the accounting department that is consistent with the views of the owner, and communicate the vision and mission to staff	
• seeking support when challenges may exceed individual competencies	• actively provide staff with coaching to enhance their individual competencies	

RESPONSIBILITIES DELEGATED TO STAFF	CORE RESPONSIBILITIES OF THE FINANCIAL CONTROLLER	RESPONSIBILITIES DELEGATED TO A CONSULTANT
• understanding the importance of being a team player	• facilitate team-building within the department and between departments	
• understanding corporate values	• embrace corporate values	

Strategic thinking and communication

One important role that the financial controller performs which adds value to the organization relates to the issue of strategic thinking and communication. The first step in the process is for the financial controller to have a clear understanding of the vision and mission of the key decision-makers. In smaller organizations, it may be necessary for the financial controller to work closely with the owners to help them to formalize their views and to communicate them to the rest of the organization.

In the second step, the financial controller would then formulate a vision and mission for the accounting department that is consistent with the overall vision and mission of the organization. The role of the accounting department vision and mission is to provide general guidance; these should be viewed as tools that empower employees.

Coaching and team-building

An important component of leadership is coaching and team-building. Effective financial controllers will allocate time to coaching staff because this will enable the delegation of more activities. Coaching should not be limited to having staff learn new procedures or gain technical knowledge, but should also include the enhancing of competencies such as motivation and interpersonal skills. Ideally, each staff member will possess an inventory of skills and competencies, and the formal program will serve to guide the further growth of the employee.

As a senior staff person, the financial controller can be a role model when participating in teams, and use this position of leadership to both facilitate group dynamics and help create effective team work. Depending on the nature of the project, the financial controller might be team leader and directly influence the behaviour of the team. In other projects, his or her role might be to provide support only. Whatever the situation, the financial controller can indirectly influence team behaviour by maintaining a positive attitude.

Corporate values

Every organization has corporate values. These are the beliefs or principles which create the corporate culture. As a professional accountant bound by a code of ethics, the financial controller can demonstrate leadership by including integrity as one of the corporate values. When an organization includes integrity as one of its values, it is much less likely that the financial controller will find him- or herself performing a corporate activity that is in violation of the code of ethics by which the individual is bound. As a long-term business strategy, including integrity as a corporate value will help ensure long-term relationships with all of its stakeholders.

External Relationships

While most organizations understand the importance of maintaining external relationships, this is probably not a "high priority" function in the estimation of most SME financial controllers. Notwithstanding, they must use a broad range of external resources in financial and other support service areas. These include the traditional areas of audit, taxation, and banking support, and extend through to the members of the Board of Directors, legal advisors, human resource specialists, and information/technology advisors. In SMEs, many of these external contacts will have a personal relationship with the owners and key managers.

The financial controller in an SME has very limited time, and it must be wisely used. Ensuring the selection and performance of key "partners" in all areas of support will allow him or her to effectively delegate tasks while spending the least amount of time in managing the process.

The following are some key external relationship functions that a financial controller must address.

RESPONSIBILITIES DELEGATED TO STAFF	CORE RESPONSIBILITIES OF THE FINANCIAL CONTROLLER	RESPONSIBILITIES DELEGATED TO A CONSULTANT
	• identify and make an inventory of external contacts	
	• develop a communication program and schedule meetings for the next year	
	• monitor performance and revise the communication program as required	

Identify and make an inventory of external contacts

The first step in the process is to identify all of the financial controller's external contacts as well as the nature of the dealings involved.

CONTACT/ACTIVITY	ISSUES TO BE ADDRESSED
External auditors • Annual statement reviews/audits and internal controls. May also act as advisors to the owners • May have had a long-term relationship with the owners, possibly even since start-up	• confidence in staff selection and internal controls • confidence in the controller and his or her relationship with owners/managers • evidence of financial planning, forecasting, and reporting • evidence of an ability to carry out plans • assurance that the issues identified in audit reports will be dealt with on a timely basis
External tax advisors • May be associated with the organization's auditors • May also have legal representation • May handle both the company's and the owner's tax planning and returns	• knowledge of related parties and the basis of transactions • full perspective on the company and the personal affairs of the owners • evidence of tax considerations being factored into key business decisions • timely completion of financials and payment of taxes due • demonstrated systems to collect and remit taxes due
Bank contacts • May be more than one contact (e.g., the account manager, branch manager, loans managers, and even specialists such as equity financing reps.)	• awareness of financial plans, budgets, and forecasts • availability of current financial results to compare against the agreed plan • regular updating of business decisions that affect cash flow
Legal firms • May carry out company "secretarial" duties (keeping minutes books, etc.) • May handle litigation as well as registration of patents, royalty agreements, etc. • May also be involved in new company set-up, mergers, acquisitions, etc. • Will often be responsible for the owner's affairs.	• compliance with acts and legislation governing companies (keeping of books, minutes, etc.) • ensuring directors' and officers' awareness of the company's liabilities/risks • notification re: the organization's plans, ventures, and potential liabilities

CONTACT/ACTIVITY	ISSUES TO BE ADDRESSED
Venture capital funds • Relevant to organizations which have equity, debt, or a convertible debt position	• generally the same as the bank contacts plus: ➤ consistency of operating results measured against strategy/plans ➤ demonstrated ability to create cash in line with plans ➤ growth strategy for making profits and game plan for creating a profitable "sell" opportunity
Board of Directors • Probably comprised of several individuals, including officers of the company and key equity holders • The controller should know the position and the background of board members, and their expectations, through working with the president, CEO, and/or chairman of the Board • Regular reporting will be key	• confidence in the management of the accounts • on-time availability of information • internal controls that result in no surprises from interim to final results • effective financial plans and forecasts • reliability of projections, including cash and debt provisions • compliance with statutory requirements (e.g., tax remittances, etc.)
Insurance organizations • May be the agent who handles the firm's regular insurance. The financial controller should ensure that this individual is providing risk analysis and management advice ➤ The organization may also need a risk management specialist	• process in place for risk recognition • internal controls enacted to limit liability (e.g., safety programs) • quality programs to minimize product/service liability • controls to minimize other losses (accidents, theft, fraud, etc.)
Computer and systems support • One or more individuals who provide back-up technical advice and support. Controllers should look for continuity in this area, as well as knowledge of the hardware configuration and all applications being run	• controlled access to hardware and software (e.g., to add software) • security measures in place for system access and data protection • recognition by management of the pace of technological change
Real estate advisors • A relationship may exist through which property is being leased or rented, either at the main facility or elsewhere	• maintenance systems for property, plant, and equipment • safety and facility protection (security systems, etc.) • advance notice of upcoming business changes, additions, etc.

CONTACT/ACTIVITY	ISSUES TO BE ADDRESSED
Collection agency/factors • The organization may have retained the services of an organization to collect overdue receivables or through which outstanding items are "factored" for cash flow management	• effective credit granting facilities • application of effective credit limits and controls • early advice re: problem areas • automated ability to transfer data on a timely basis
Consulting organizations • May be a number of consulting organizations, each focusing on a specific area (which the controller should be aware of). This includes strategic planning, human resources, compensation planning, quality and service management, and others	• clear definition of tasks, roles, and responsibilities • clear communication of needs, requirements, and issues/problems • integrity in using and sharing data and methodologies
Benefits, pensions/actuarials • May be one or more advisors for benefits and a pension plan — some to advise on the structure, and others to administer the plan, carry out valuations, and manage investments • Good performance measures and tracking are important	• effective human resource management systems (pay structure, ranges, performance reviews, and documented action plans) • verification that your assumptions concerning interest rates, the rate of inflation, cost of living, demographics, etc., are realistic
Outsourcing • May include typical activities such as payroll, as well as logistics management and other services • Performance measurement is a key issue	• clearly defined responsibility and performance criteria • effective sharing and communication of key information • timeliness of transactional data, where relevant • established policies and procedures for dealing with any perceived or real conflict of interest associated with third-party agreements
Key customer and supplier contacts • Maintaining a working relationship with critical/key suppliers and with significant customers is an important aspect of the controller's role in an SME	• clear communication of commercial data (e.g., payments, billings, etc.) • communication of business changes that affect them • availability of points of contact for problem resolution • relationship thinking (i.e., adopting a long-term perspective) • integrity of words and deeds, and follow-up on promises made

Develop a communication program and schedule meetings for the next year

The second step in the process is to assign responsibility for the various types of meetings, and then to prepare a formal schedule indicating when they are due to be held.

Financial controllers must maintain clear communication with external contacts, ensuring that the relationship adds value from both partners' perspectives. Upholding these relationships will often create situations for the financial controller where good time management and personal communication skills are needed, and even situations when ethical issues may arise. In making the process work, it is important that controllers understand the relationship and act as a "team member", showing consideration for others who may be involved or indirectly affected by it.

The following are points to keep in mind when planning for meetings with external contacts.

- Establish clear expectations between the two organizations by designating the performance standards. Use these criteria to measure activity and review performance at least once a year. Make sure that the expectations concerning administrative details are also defined and documented (e.g., term of agreements, types of work, billing and payment rates, taxes, etc.).

- Take corrective action as a financial controller when problems occur.

- Do not keep changing suppliers and support resources; both the buyer and the seller make an investment in creating a relationship in the first place, and the best way to ensure a beneficial return on investment (ROI) is to build a long-term relationship (based on performance standards discussed in the preceding table); create a mutually beneficial "partnering" type of relationship.

- Communicate on a regular basis. Methods vary, but could include regular email exchanges, copying key contacts on press releases and applicable internal notices and changes, holding regular briefing meetings, etc. Have several contacts in the partner firm to ensure continuity if one person leaves or is promoted.

- Involve outside contacts in some internal activities or social events so that they can increase their level of knowledge about your business and establish contacts.

- Share knowledge with outside contacts. Some organizations hold briefing meetings on a quarterly basis, so that key consultants from different organizations can come together and turn potential conflict situations into co-operative ones.

- Be proactive to avoid surprises and conflicts. Recognize that your partners' or suppliers' agendas may not match yours and issues must be brought forward and addressed.

Monitor performance and revise the communication program, as required

The last step in the process requires that the financial controller objectively review, on a periodic basis, all activities related to maintaining external relationships, and determine whether any changes need to be made, e.g., changing the timing of meetings or increasing their frequency.

Chapter 5

Checking: Building a Performance Measurement System

Summary ☞

Performance monitoring is a key aspect of effective controllership. This chapter identifies the importance of both financial and non-financial performance measurement. The alignment of the measurement system with "planning" and "doing" is discussed, from which effective management action can result. The importance of using information technology is also addressed. The section ends with a discussion of the controller's role in broad compliance reporting.

Reporting and information management is another task traditionally viewed as the responsibility of the financial controller. As a result, financial controllers must implement processes and develop tools and methods that communicate information about the business in a way that is readily understood. The financial controller must not only present results as they occur, but also be able to clearly link these results to the actions and activities taking place in the business. In effect, the financial controller must be a communicator, reporter, and translator all in one.

Reporting and information management tasks can be broken down into three main functions as follows:

REPORTING AND INFORMATION MANAGEMENT	HOURS PER YEAR	ASSIGNMENT OF RESPONSIBILITIES BY THE FINANCIAL CONTROLLER
Reporting, monitoring, and control management	310	The financial controller: • assigns day-to-day administration • plans, develops, and implements reporting and monitoring procedures • reviews and interprets reports • plans, develops, and implements control procedures • may seek the support of an external consultant
Information technology and communication management	75	The financial controller: • assigns day-to-day administration • develops medium-term plans for maintenance/revision of systems • may seek the support of an external consultant
Regulation and tax administration	60	The financial controller: • assigns day-to-day administration • develops schedules • reviews all processes and ensures that they are completed on time • may seek the support of external consultants

In some organizations, for the company to maintain a competitive advantage, information technology is continually being updated. If such is the case, the financial controller may have to allocate many more hours to IT and information management.

Financial Reporting, Monitoring, and Control Management

The following are some key functions that a financial controller must address:

RESPONSIBILITIES DELEGATED TO STAFF	CORE RESPONSIBILITIES OF THE FINANCIAL CONTROLLER	RESPONSIBILITIES DELEGATED TO A CONSULTANT
• day-to-day administration of financial reporting	• understand the different information and reporting requirements of the various stakeholders	• verify the financial controller's interpretation of GAAP
• understanding the role of various activities in providing control	• maintain one's body of knowledge regarding the application of GAAP	• review the efficiency and effectiveness of internal control
	• implement a schedule and procedures for reporting	
	• review and interpret reports	
	• implement internal control procedures	
	• review the efficiency and effectiveness of internal control	

Understand the different information and reporting requirements of the various stakeholders

For the financial controller, the starting point in this process is to recognize that different stakeholders have different information and reporting requirements. Consequently, all stakeholders must be identified as well as the types of information they require, using formal and/or informal means.

The financial controller should then assess whether the information supplied to stakeholders does in fact address their specific needs. If necessary, the information may need to be revised.

It is important to appreciate that information extends beyond financial data and operational output. In recent years, recognition has grown that a number of other reports on business activities can be as valuable to decision-makers as financial information. The financial controller who has a firm grasp of organizational activities and understands the key "drivers" of the firm will be able to identify the critical pieces of financial and non-financial information to supply.

Maintain one's body of knowledge concerning the application of GAAP and understand the reporting requirements of the various regulatory agencies

Accounting standards are currently undergoing a revolution as the world moves towards a consistent set of statements dealing with underlying accounting treatments (IAS) as well as financial reporting (IFRS). While this process will eventually result in greater consistency, the changes may well result in significant issues that controllers must address. The breadth and depth of such standards is significant, and controllers are advised not only to make themselves aware, but also to work closely with their financial advisors to assess the implications and develop effective strategies to deal with issues. Examples of potentially significant impacts include the "fair value" approaches, which can call for impairment assessments of assets on an organization's balance sheet such that idle capacity (of fixed assets) may result in write-downs of balance sheet values.

Preparing financial reporting to provide the information required to satisfy various regulatory requirements such as tax reporting has always been a primary function of the financial controller. With improvements in information processing, demands have become much less onerous, freeing up the financial controller to focus more on issues such as the interpretation of Generally Accepted Accounting Principles (GAAP).

Since financial reporting is one of the primary functions of the financial controller, it is important that his or her knowledge of GAAP remains current. This demand may be significantly greater or more complex in the case of organizations with independent subsidiaries in foreign countries.

It is also important for the financial controller to remain current as concerns the reporting requirements of various government agencies. Changes in reporting requirements may mean instituting significant modifications to the systems currently in place for the company to gather and/or report information.

Implement a schedule and procedures for reporting

In order for the financial controller to be able to successfully delegate the day-to-day administration of financial reporting, it is important that all of the organization's procedures related to reporting be formalized. Creating and instituting such documentation will reduce opportunities for misunderstandings to occur as to what specific processes should be followed.

The second step is for the financial controller to develop a schedule for all activities related to reporting, taking into account that in order to meet certain deadlines, lead time may have to be factored in to receive feedback from staff in other departments. In preparing a schedule, it is important for the financial controller to balance the trade-off between the timeliness of information required and its accuracy.

Review and interpret reports

The financial controller should not underestimate the importance of reviewing various reports. Moreover, in completing the review process, he or she will be wearing a number of different hats. The first step is to determine whether all of the major activities and transactions that have occurred in the past year are in fact reflected in the various reports. Secondly, in reviewing the reports, the financial controller should be looking for "yellow flags", or indicators that problems may occur if some action is not taken. For example, if a company report announces that the marketing force has secured long-term contracts to deliver 40% more of a product in the new year, the financial controller should recognize that this will place new demands on the firm's working capital requirements. For example, increased lines of credit, both from raw material suppliers and the bank, may be needed.

On a periodic basis, the financial controller must also step back and critically assess the value of reports.

- Is the information in the report in a format that is easily understood?

- Is there too much or too little information? Does the report focus on key issues?

- Is the information timely?

- Is the report being provided to the stakeholders who need the information it contains?

- What are the lost opportunities? What costs are incurred if the report is not provided?

Implement internal control procedures

The implementation of internal control procedures could be viewed as a means to minimize various types of risks associated with the management of the organization's assets and liabilities. One group of internal control procedures is designed to protect the integrity of the information that is recorded. A second group of internal control procedures is designed to protect the actual assets and liabilities of the organization.

In designing internal control procedures, the financial controller must consider the trade-off between the cost of implementing a given control and the potential loss that could occur if it were not implemented. It is also important to understand that there may be more than one way to implement an internal control feature.

The financial controller will face a number of interesting challenges in trying to implement internal control in the SME environment. For example, segregation of duties is often suggested as a key component of internal control. Unfortunately, in an SME, there may not be a sufficient amount of a given type of work to justify this type of control. A second example often found in SMEs is that authority is concentrated in the hands of one or two owners who may give directives to staff that defeat internal control features. In both examples, the financial controller will have to find procedures to protect the resources of the organization.

Review the efficiency and effectiveness of internal control

On a periodic basis, the financial controller should review the efficiency and effectiveness of the internal control. He or she should verify that documented policies and procedures are in fact being observed. He or she should also review various reports and transactions for irregularities. In so doing, the financial controller is, in effect, playing the role of forensic accountant, but it is important not to create the perception that the organization does not trust its employees. For this reason, the review of internal control functions is often delegated to external consultants.

The Controller's Role in Broad-Based Performance Measurement

Effective controllers who work as a part of the organization's management team will play a key role in ensuring that both financial and non-financial measures form the basis for management reporting. In the years since *The Balanced Scorecard* was written, increasing numbers of organizations have been moving to management reporting systems that include financial information as well as key client/customer/market information, internal management data (project and process monitoring and measures), and human resource indicators. Such approaches ensure that:

- Performance measures are developed during the planning process
- Chosen measures reflect key strategic aspects of plan achievement
- High-level outcome measures reflect business objectives
- Measures are capable of being "de-composed" from objectives to operational strategies that can be monitored
- Emphasis on monitoring is on exception reporting

- Every measure has a linked management accountability (who is responsible?)

- Key measures are often compared to "best practice" benchmarks

- The measures chosen typically combine aspects of leading and lagging indicators (history and future indicators)

- Measures may be both objective and subjective (i.e., such as definitive outputs measures or survey responses)

- Measures are often presented in a "dashboard" approach, providing a high-level summary

- Red, green and amber colours are often used on measures to indicate problem issues, items on or ahead of plan, and items to be watched.

Importance to Controller of non-financial measures

While in many cases non-financial areas may represent performance from other functional areas of the organization such as human resources, sales, marketing and operations, the controller has a vested interest in understanding their linkage with financial performance. Typically, financial data represents outcomes after they have been achieved; however in today's fast-paced environment, early warning signs need to be developed. As an example, while revenue reporting will show sales outcomes, measures such as backlog, order entry levels, client satisfaction, process performance (in areas such as on-time delivery), and even economic trends can provide indicators of possible impending changes in revenue potential. The controller should work with other members of the management team to determine what the strategic linkages are between "activities" and outcomes, and from this, strive to develop a broad-based performance measures framework that balances financial information with information about the day-to-day work that ultimately drives the financial results.

Process measures are of particular interest to the controller. Processes are the building blocks of organizational activity — whether in accounting (such as payables process, billing process, and reporting process) or anywhere else in the organization. In manufacturing, the processes will be those necessary to convert materials into finished products (often well defined through manufacturing work breakdown structures and work flows). In non-manufacturing organizations, it might be processes required to convert an insurance claim to a settlement, or to process a loan application. In government, it might be the process to assess tax return or complete a taxpayer audit. What is important to the controller is that every one of these processes determines how many resources are required to complete the work. Knowing process cycle times, accuracy rates, volumes of transactions being processed, and, in particular, the cost per transaction, provides valuable information to the controller about what is driving organizational costs and where opportunities for improvement may exist. Effective financial management will be attempting to align financial analysis with operational activity, and in many cases this might involve the controller exploring tools, such as Activity Based Costing (ABC) or Resource Consumption Accounting (RCA), or some aspect of these approaches that allows more effective cost collection and reporting from the general ledger.

Information Technology and Communication Management

One of the greatest challenges for an SME is the management of information technology and communication, and in most cases, the financial controller will play a central role. Judicious investments in information technology and communication can result in a competitive advantage for the company while reducing labour costs and integrating the flow of information.

Financial controllers may be required to manage information technology and communication processes, and to advise owners of the decisions that have to be taken. But if they are to make efficient and effective use of their time, they should focus on understanding key issues and consider seeking the support of specialists to provide detailed advice and support.

The following are some key IT and communication management functions that a financial controller must address:

RESPONSIBILITIES DELEGATED TO STAFF	CORE RESPONSIBILITIES OF THE FINANCIAL CONTROLLER	RESPONSIBILITIES DELEGATED TO A CONSULTANT
• requirement to have a working knowledge of policies and procedures related to information technology and communication	• review current policies related to information technology and communication	• consult specialists on the implementation of information technology and strategic communication goals to gain a competitive advantage
	• review current hardware/software systems	

RESPONSIBILITIES DELEGATED TO STAFF	CORE RESPONSIBILITIES OF THE FINANCIAL CONTROLLER	RESPONSIBILITIES DELEGATED TO A CONSULTANT
	• identify opportunities to improve procedures and systems	
	• develop long-term plans for information technology and communication	
	• remain current on developments affecting information technology and communication	

Review current policies related to information technology and communication

One of the first tasks that a financial controller should perform is a review of the organization's policies and procedures related to information technology and communication.

It might be argued that, in an SME, formal policies and procedures have limited value. On the other hand, any organization that has lost one or two key employees in a short period of time would argue that having documented policies and procedures is a form of insurance that the organization cannot afford to be without.

Some policies and procedures to consider formalizing are identified as follows:

REVIEW OF POLICIES RELATED TO INFORMATION TECHNOLOGY AND COMMUNICATION

POLICIES AND PROCEDURES	OBSERVATION	ACTION REQUIRED (Y/N)
Capital expenditures • Is there a formally-documented process for authorizing the purchase of hardware/software related to information technology and communication?		

POLICIES AND PROCEDURES	OBSERVATION	ACTION REQUIRED (Y/N)
• Is there a dollar threshold which requires the approval of the owner/Board? • Has responsibility for such purchases been assigned to specific individuals?		
Operations • Are there formal policies and procedures in place related to documentation? ➤ process descriptions, including internal control; ➤ applications manuals; ➤ databases description; ➤ scheduling of processes. • Are there policies and procedures for maintenance and back-up? ➤ hardware; ➤ software; ➤ data; ➤ staff. • Are there policies and procedures for recovery of critical data and systems in the event of a disaster?		
Security • Are there policies and procedures ensuring the physical security of the hardware and software related to information technology and communication? • Are there policies and procedures covering access to systems and data? ➤ Are passwords issued and required for access to computer work stations, telephones, and fax machines?		

POLICIES AND PROCEDURES	OBSERVATION	ACTION REQUIRED (Y/N)
• Are employees aware of policies and procedures related to the security of information technology and communication? What about: ➤ installing of unauthorized programs? ➤ securing of passwords?		

Review current hardware and software systems

Financial controllers should carry out a "health check" on their current level of reliance in information technology and communication. This should include creating an inventory of all software and hardware being used. The following are some key items to consider:

REVIEW OF HARDWARE AND SOFTWARE RELATED TO INFORMATION TECHNOLOGY AND COMMUNICATION

ITEM TO BE ADDRESSED	OBSERVATION	ACTION REQUIRED (Y/N)
Hardware • Review all hardware — ➤ networks; ➤ computers; ➤ telephones; ➤ fax machines. • Review all costs associated with hardware. • Identify hardware that is critical to the organization. • Estimate the useful life of hardware.		

ITEM TO BE ADDRESSED	OBSERVATION	ACTION REQUIRED (Y/N)

Software
 	
• Review all software —
 	
  ➢ operating system;
 	
  ➢ applications;
 	
  ➢ are there any legacy systems?
 	
• Review all costs associated with software —
 	
  ➢ updating and maintenance costs;
 	
  ➢ training costs.
 	
• Review the degree of integration
 	
  ➢ of systems within the organization at the same location;
 	
  ➢ of systems within the organization at different locations;
 	
  ➢ with systems outside the organization.
 	
• Estimate the useful life of software.
 	
• Identify software that is critical to the organization.		

Identify opportunities to improve procedures and systems

The financial controller can add value to the organization by identifying opportunities to improve procedures and systems that will enable the organization to achieve its strategic goals in a more efficient or effective manner. Opportunities include the following categories:

- reducing operating costs;

- improving the quality of information for decision-making;

- improving the flow of information.

Develop long-term plans for information technology and communication

The organization's investment in information technology and communication can be significant, and it is possible to spread expenditures over a longer period of time by using long-term planning. However, given the rapid rate at which IT change occurs, it is important to build in flexibility concerning the selection of hardware and software in the event that unforeseen purchases seem wise to make in the future.

In developing long-term plans, it is also important to make provisions for staff training.

Remain current on developments affecting information technology and communication

Finally, it is important that the financial controller remain current on new developments affecting information technology and communication. Because of the rapidity of change in this sector, the financial controller should update his or her knowledge on a regular basis, and focus on discerning what the latest trends are and how they might apply in the context of the organization. In some organizations, the issue may be sufficiently critical to warrant a review by external consultants every three or four years. Examples of ways to keep current on developments in information technology include:

- attending hardware/software trade shows;

- attending seminars and workshops;

- scanning information technology trade journals;

- networking with peers.

Regulation and Tax Administration

In addition to the administration associated with payroll and different types of taxes, the financial controller should be prepared to respond to a wide variety of requests. Some regulations will require administrative support on a regular basis, whereas other types may require the financial controller's attention only if some unusual event occurs.

The following are some key administrative functions that a financial controller must perform in relation to tax and regulatory matters:

RESPONSIBILITIES DELEGATED TO STAFF	CORE RESPONSIBILITIES OF THE FINANCIAL CONTROLLER	RESPONSIBILITIES DELEGATED TO A CONSULTANT
● day-to-day administrative activities related to regulatory and tax administration	● identify all of the regulations which the organization will have to comply with	● use consultants for specialized activities
	● prepare a schedule of activities	
	● assign responsibilities	
	● review all information that will be filed with regulatory agencies	
	● remain current on regulatory and tax administration requirements	

Identify all of the regulations which the organization will have to comply with

The financial controller should begin by identifying all of the regulations that the organization will have to comply with. He or she must consider not only federal regulations but also the requirements of provincial and local regulatory bodies.

In many cases, the organization is acting as an agent in collecting taxes or miscellaneous fees such as payroll remittances, GST/HST, and provincial sales taxes. These are everyday routines which are part of the organization's compliance process. There are also various regulations that necessitate a response only if some unusual activity occurs. For example, in the event of certain types of equipment failure, there may be environmental regulations in place requiring the immediate reporting of the event. While such activities are not part of standard procedures, it is important that the organization be able to comply with the applicable regulations.

Prepare a schedule of activities

The financial controller should then prepare a schedule of the activities that the organization must perform in order to be in compliance with the various regulations which affect it, and highlight any particular input that may be required from specific departments. In addition, the financial controller may want to flag activities that will incur penalties in the event of late filings. Examples of some activities that could be included on the schedule are:

- annual company filing;

- income tax instalments and filing;

- GST instalments and filing;

- sales tax filing;

- payroll remittances, T4s, T4 summaries;

- local business licence renewal.

Assign responsibilities

There should be documentation that identifies what responsibilities have been assigned overall — and to which person or post — for ensuring that the organization is in compliance with each regulation affecting it. The documentation should be explicit as to the nature of the responsibility, the accuracy of the data to be provided, and the timeliness required for the filing.

In assigning responsibility, the organization has to decide whether it is efficient or effective for the administrative activity to be assigned to staff or whether it should be outsourced. In the event that the responsibility is assigned to an employee of the organization, it is important that other staff be trained to act in a back-up capacity.

Review all information that will be filed with regulatory agencies

Even though the responsibility for administration associated with regulatory requirements may be assigned to staff within the department, the financial controller should review all filings before they are submitted. Having an overall view of the organization, he or she may quickly spot errors or omissions in the filing. In addition, the financial controller is often one of the signing officers of the organization, and performing such a review is a simple matter of prudence.

Remain current on regulatory and tax administration requirements

Last but not least, the financial controller must implement a process that will enable him or her to remain up to date on changes in regulations that may affect the organization. Several methods can be used to stay up to date, such as:

- receiving communications (e.g., newsletters) from consultants;
- subscribing to services;
- attending conferences/workshops;
- networking with peers.

Chapter 6

Fact-Based Decision Making for Taking Action

Summary ☞

The goal of the Plan, Do, Check, and Act (PDCA) management model is to ensure effective deployment of organizational resources in a way that results in the planned outcomes being achieved. In this chapter, the "Act" portion of the model is discussed. The purpose of reporting is to ensure that managers and other key stakeholders can assess progress against anticipated outcomes. If results fall short of expectations, corrective action must be taken either to improve execution or modify plans. If results indicate that plans are "on track", reporting acts as a "health check" and allows managers to continue. Effective approaches to problem solving are discussed as an important aspect of aligning "out of control" measures to operational problems and then to effective root-cause solutions. Finally, a checklist is provided to help controllers focus on implementation of key tools.

Alignment of Reporting and Action

Data supplied by the controller to operational managers is only of value if it is clear, concise, simple, timely, and, most importantly, aligned with the manager's actual responsibilities. The only way to achieve the latter goal is for the controller to spend time with line managers, understand their operational activities, and discuss and develop the type of reporting that will add value. Controllers typically have strong analytical thinking skills, which can help managers identify linkages between what they do and what reporting will support it.

In addition to defining types of reporting and report content, the controller should work with managers to ascertain their learning strengths. Through this, the controller can identify the type of presentation format that will communicate information in the most effective and easily understood manner.

The amount of value the controller adds to any organization will be greatly influenced by the level of support the line managers receive. It is in this role that the controller can provide the greatest impact on business results. Controllers should always ask themselves whether the information they are providing highlights the most important issues that managers need to act upon.

Two points will illustrate this: Firstly, traditional responsibility accounting for financial data (i.e., based on cost centres/responsibility centres that align with the organization chart and with the manager's accountability) has worked well to identify what money is being spent (i.e., by GL expense code) and who is spending it. However, in today's environment, a more valuable question might be "why are we spending this?" This raises questions about causal analysis and spending drivers. Current management thinking places much greater emphasis on understanding business processes as the building blocks of organizational activity — yet in many organizations, financial reporting does not provide this type of data. Process thinking is the fundamental approach to management behind quality management, cycle time management, value chain management, lean management, six sigma process design, development and process FMEA (Failure Mode and Effect Analysis), and many others — yet costs are often not aligned with process. More effective organizations have started to deploy activity-based thinking, which starts to create this alignment. More advanced financial tools and systems allow activity reporting to become a key component of cost collection architecture, but again, not many organizations develop and deploy this capability on an effective organization-wide basis. If managers are focusing on the performance of business processes, shouldn't financial data be presented in the same way?

Secondly, it has been known for over forty years by those in the quality movement that there is a cost to poor quality. Books, articles, and cases have been written and presented on the subject by organizations such as the American Society for Quality. The impact of poor process quality could be significant — with projections ranging between 10% and 40% of total costs being wasted. Many controllers admit that they know waste such as this is actually taking place within their own organizations, yet when asked "how much does this actually cost you?" almost no one can answer. If any controller believes that waste exists because things "don't work right" in their organization, then they should strive to develop financial reporting that highlights such information so that management can take action on it. While some of the figures may not be exact, they will help to identify a key cost reduction opportunity, and while results from improvements and savings may not immediately drop to the bottom line, such knowledge and the resulting action will help to develop a continually improving operation that in turn will build competitive advantage or allow "not-for-profit" organizations to make more effective use of limited resources. The following chart shows the potential implication of such knowledge and actions:

Checklist for Effective "Acting"

Issue	Result				Action
	OK	NI	NA	NR	
Organization has effective planning in place					
KPIs have been developed for the organization					
KPIs have been decomposed into aligned operational measures					
Clear accountability exists for all operational measures (ownership)					
Performance limits have been set for key operational measures					
Rapid reporting of actual results against limits has been established					
Visual indicators have been established (red, amber, green)					
Managers have been given drill down capability to access underlying performance information					
Statistical tools have been developed to allow analysis of key process/project performance					

Issue	Result				Action
	OK	NI	NA	NR	
Managers have been trained in statistical tools and techniques					
Controller has developed financial training for other managers					
Operational simulations to show financial impact have been developed					
Controller has identified core drivers of resource consumption					
Controller has identified core aspects of wasted resources due to poor quality					
Cost of poor quality has been included in regular reporting					
"Real/actual" cost reporting is available in real time					
Lean management techniques have been investigated and applied where practical					
Target costs for key products, services, and process are set					
Continual improvement is practised as a core management approach					
The implications of human productivity in all work areas is identified and measured					
Organization has adopted a framework for structured problem solving					
Managers have been trained in structured problem solving framework					
Managers have been trained in supporting techniques (brainstorming, fishbone, etc.)					
Experiences in effective problem solving are identified and shared					

Key to chart OK = Acceptable; NI = Needs Improvement; NA = Not Acceptable
(Must have actions attached); NR = Not Required/Not Relevant.

Process Cost Improvement Leverage

Cost in thousands	Earnings statement	Cost of poor quality	Real cost of operations	Revised percentages	Future opportunity
Revenues	$100		$100	100.0%	$111
Costs — labour	$ 60	$6	$ 54	54.0%	$ 60
Costs — other	$ 20	$2	$ 18	18.0%	$ 20
Gross margin	$ 20		$ 28	28.0%	$ 31
Interest and other	$ 5		$ 5	5.0%	$ 5
Taxation	$ 7		$ 9	9.0%	$ 10
Return on revenue	$ 8		$ 14	14.0%	$ 16

In this example, "business as usual" reflects a profit of $8 on sales of $100 with other costs as shown; however, included in these costs are "wasted" resources caused by poor quality in the amounts of $6 in labour and $2 in other expenses. If these were not being incurred, the "real cost" of today's operations would be $8 lower, and after-tax profits would be $6 higher. This would result in the potential percentages of costs and returns being higher; however, many CEOs would argue that savings from "parts of people" cannot result in bottom line improvements — it would also mean that an organization could grow its revenues by 11% (to $111) without any increase in operating costs, resulting in a doubling of after-tax profits. Not a small opportunity (to achieve the same after-tax result without making these improvements would mean having to double sales).

Controller as Trainer and Educator

An effective controller goes beyond understanding the activities of other line managers, and becomes a coach and supporter to achieve an improved understanding of financial reporting across the organization. Controllers should recognize that, for many non-accountants, financial data and reporting can be complicated, overwhelming, and confusing. The controller plays a key role in helping managers understand the connection between the aspects of what they actually manage and the impact that their decisions have on financial performance.

One of the most effective approaches is to create cost and investment simulations; using these, managers can modify key decision points and quickly see the impact on financial results. For example, in an industrial distribution business, each manager runs his or her branch as an autonomous business unit, yet the combined results of each manager's decisions define the overall organizational performance. Simulations can be created to demonstrate the impact of:

(a) Gross margin improvements through modifications to customer mix (number of larger and smaller accounts), product mix (types of items being sold), margin management (ability to sustain targeted levels of pricing by product), and strategies to charge extra costs rather than absorbing them (e.g., freight costs for client deliveries);

(b) Cost improvements by changing selling strategies, such as increasing average order size (number of items per sales order and dollar value per sales order), and improvements to process quality through elimination of errors and the resulting need to replace deliveries free of charge;

(c) Improvements in cost performance through identification of core processes and development of simplified approaches in areas such as order fulfilment. Although this might start with automation of order taking through implementation of either Internet-based ordering or EDI, it can just as easily yield improvements through simplification of manual processes (using standard forms, re-organizing inventory to reduce travel time to pick orders, simplification of billing and shipping);

(d) Improvements to return on investment (ROI) through more effective target selling of core stocked items (improvements in inventory turnover rates); this might involve implementation of inventory stratification and setting/controlling service levels by category (e.g., "A" items — 100% fill rate, 0 back orders; this might also reduce the impact of areas such as unabsorbed freight costs due to having to ship "part orders" to clients);

(e) Improvements in AR (working capital reductions and interest rate cost reductions) through more effective processes for order entry, shipping, and billing (fewer errors), as well as taking action to reduce the number of days AR are outstanding by implementing improved sales follow-up procedures.

All of these and possibly more can be developed using "what if" scenarios that reflect the impact of improved management of key business activities. Results may not be seen immediately; however, such planning will demonstrate to the manager what areas he or she should concentrate on, and the benefits of doing so.

In addition to these planning activities, the controller should also spend time ensuring that "actual" financial reporting information is understood by line managers in a way that allows them to connect "outcomes" with their "actions"; in this way, they will enhance their ability to drive improvement. Such discussions will also allow the controller to better understand the role and responsibility of the line managers, as well as to help ensure that financial reporting is constantly being enhanced and improved in a way that it is client focused.

Using Fact-Based Decision Making

A key outcome of this focus on line managers as "clients" will be the development of their management skills. The phrase "fact-based management" has become popular in recent years and is being further developed through focus on analytics. While this might appear logical to most readers, many experienced controllers will know that in the absence of clear and effective financial (and other operational) facts and information, managers tend to make decisions "by the seat of their pants". While intuitive decision making is valid and will continually to be used in cases where experienced managers are trading off risks of less than 100% available information against the risk of not making a decision based on what information is available (typically what an effective entrepreneur does), the focus on getting the right information to the right people at the right time will enhance their ability to base decisions on as many facts as possible.

Every organization is faced with increasing challenges from more difficult economic conditions; public sector organizations (and not-for-profit organizations) have increasing demands for funds and programs, especially those facing the demographic impact of increased aging; yet, global competitiveness demands that governments at every level limit and reduce taxation to create a more effective environment to allow businesses to compete internationally. Private sector organizations face competition through the impact of global communications, allowing clients access to product and service acquisition through the Internet from anywhere in the world. Whole sectors of commercial infrastructure are being eliminated as providers, and end users are brought together without the need for retailers (e.g., Amazon) or third-party distribution. Knowledge experts are being replaced by the wiki approach to collaboration and information sharing. Manufacturing is being shifted to "lowest cost" sources around the world. Today, even greater dislocation is starting to occur as energy costs soar to unprecedented levels, creating yet another shift. Every one of these changes is making the need for fast, high-quality information ever more critical. The controller must play a key role in ensuring that not only is speed and accuracy addressed but also that the principles being used are aligned with operational reality and reflect operationally correct information. In practical terms, what does this require from the controller?

- Organizations who do not know which processes drive the demand for and consume corporate resources cannot advise management effectively on cost management and reduction; process-based thinking is critical;

- Organizations need to know and focus on real costs aligned with real decision making; in many cases, this means throwing out traditional approaches to operational management and costing, and adopting lean management together with "real time" actual cost-based reporting, coupled with target costing and continual improvement. (The book *The Toyota Way*[1] should be required reading for every financial manager);

- Controllers who know that waste occurs in their organization through poor "quality" of performance (estimates of waste through poor quality vary from 5% to 40% of total costs), yet do not make this cost-impact identification a central part of financial reporting, are failing management by not focusing attention on key areas for improvement.

- Controllers who fail to develop financial reporting systems to measure the productivity of people in every aspect of business (today the greatest cost in most organizations) are again failing to show management where improvement opportunities occur. (Billions of dollars are poured into information technology, yet in many organizations this continues to fail to enhance productivity to the level possible, because the impact on human productivity is not being effectively monitored and reported).

The key here is that, to make the right decisions in a fiercely competitive world, managers need the facts; they need them on a timely basis, at an adequate level of detail relative to their decision making — but most of all, they need them aligned with what they manage and how they make decisions.

Use of Analytical Tools and Reports

In order to act effectively, managers need analytical data; adoption of approaches such as the following is important to drive effective use of information:

- Identification of KPIs (Key Performance Indicators) within the organization, right from high-level objectives through to aligned and linked measures and indicators at the operational level (process and project focused);

- Development of "one page reporting" approaches using tools such as the "corporate dashboard" (Balanced Scorecard), combined with "warning light" approaches (e.g., red, amber, green);

---

[1] *The Toyota Way: 14 Management Principles from the World's Greatest Manufacturer*, by Jeffrey K. Liker; McGraw-Hill Professional, 2004.

- Focus on exception reporting by:

  (a) using performance limits to drive the "warning lights" so that management attention is immediately drawn to both "out of control" (red) situations and "warning" (amber) situations, and

  (b) limiting reporting at all levels to only that which identifies variations to planned results and also through providing managers with "data mining" tools to access supporting information to high level variance reports (often referred to as "drill down" capability);

- Adoption and implementation of statistical approaches to process and cost management as well as analysis of variances (this could include establishing "control limits" on process deviations, leading to application of SPC (Statistical Process Control), adopting of sampling to balance verification costs with adequate controls, and others);

The message here is to ensure focus, focus, and focus. Managers' attention must be directed quickly to the issues requiring action; confirmation that performance is on-track is good but less critical than a rapid response to what needs correction.

Approaches to Structured Problem Solving

Finally — after the right information is made available for managers to act — how should they act? Controllers must ensure that their organizations adopt both "fact-based management" as well as "structured decision making". The latter provides a basis for managers to take the information being provided, identify root causes for deviations to plans, and then to analyze the situation effectively to take the appropriate actions. All too often in an organization's focus on "action", managers are tempted to just "change something" in their desire to fix the problem. Inadequate time or an ineffective approach to defining what action needs to be taken will lead to repeated efforts to correct "out of control" situations.

Experienced organizations have developed sophisticated approaches to problem solving (and again, approaches such as these are at the root of the success of organizations such as Toyota). While many of these can be quite overwhelming initially because of all the steps and actions involved, most are based on a fundamental six-step process, shown below:

Collect data	Define problem	Assess causes	Determine root cause	List potential solutions	Choose solution

This approach to problem solving has been widely used in the quality management movement yet has value across all aspects of organizational activity. The six steps cover:

- Collect data: this has been discussed in some depth in dialogues about reporting but would include the analytical data obtained through "drilling down" into the situation being investigated;

- Define problem: using the data obtained, a problem statement can be developed that focuses not on the measure itself but on the operational issue that caused the measure to indicate a deviation (this is a core concept: we are not fixing the measure — we are seeking to fix the underlying problem);

- Assess causes: once the problem is defined, techniques such as brainstorming, and cause and effect diagrams (fishbone, Ishikawa charts) can be used to identify all the possible causes of the operational problem;

- Determine root cause: from the "assess causes" step, one or more hypotheses can then be developed to explain the "root cause" — this being the underlying problem that needs to be fixed;

- List potential solutions: once agreement is reached on the root cause, then the wisdom of staff within the organization as well as expert advisors can be used to identify what action should be taken to correct the root cause; then finally,

- Choose solution: after the deliberation of the above step, a decision is made to focus change on one key aspect of existing operational activity. It is this decision that becomes the basis for acting to bring the situation back under control.

While many managers may find this approach frustrating, it has been proven that spending more time in up-front thinking will deliver more effective solutions. Savings will be achieved through increasing the probability that the right issue has been addressed (problem clearly defined), that the core underlying cause has been identified (root cause defined), and that the best action has been taken to address the issue (chosen solution). In addition, even if this action fails to deliver the desired results, the relationship between cause and effect of the changes will have been clearly identified. The result will be that confusion will be eliminated from those traditional situations when several things are changed and then when the solution either fails to work or works partially (or even fully), no one really knows what exactly it was that created the improvement. This effects a further "out-of-control" situation.

Extensive books and courses have been written on structured problem solving, and controllers are encouraged to become more aware of these techniques. Effective adoption of the combination of fact-based management, together with effective problem solving, will ensure that the "acting" portion of the management cycle is managed effectively.

Chapter 7

Special Situations

Summary ☞

Controllers are often involved in somewhat unique situations that can provide specific challenges that must be planned for and guarded against. This final chapter identifies several key situations that new or existing controllers may find themselves in, each requiring consideration of all materials in this handbook, but also requiring specific areas of attention. Typically, the first controllership position will require some rapid learning. There may also be specific challenges for those who choose to provide controllership services on a part-time basis, possibly to several organizations that are still at an early development stage and cannot yet justify a full-time position. Controllers in new enterprises as well as those in a family business will also face unique challenges that are discussed here.

Financial controllers may find themselves dealing with a number of special situations that merit discussion.

First Tasks of a New Financial Controller

In every organization, there will be turnover of personnel. When a new person takes over the role of financial controller, there are a number of tasks he or she should undertake in the first three weeks.

As a new financial controller, it is important to take inventory of the systems, processes, procedures, agreements, and other items already in place. It is also important to understand the short-term and long-term needs of the business and, if applicable, of the owner/manager. Making such an inventory will help to preclude unhappy surprises from occurring at a later date, and will help the new financial controller to "get up to speed" quickly and become an effective member of the management team. The following checklist is broken into broad sections to illustrate some of the main concerns that a new financial controller will encounter:

- Owners' and key managers' issues and expectations;

- Obligations and commitments that may already be in place;

- External relationships:

  ➤ legal and contractual arrangements that the financial controller should be aware of,

  ➤ supply arrangements and relationships that may be in place,

  ➤ auditing, accounting, tax planning, and management issues, etc.;

- Job function issues:

  ➤ processing issues — What processes are in place? Who does what tasks?

  ➤ reporting issues — What reports are generated? By whom? For whom? When?;

- Customers: Who are the key customers? Where they are? What is their history?

- Administration: What office management arrangements are in place?

- Human resource administration: This covers many areas. For example, what benefit plans are in place, etc.

(NOTE: Space is provided at the end of the New Controller Initial Checklist, Exhibit 7-A in Appendix II, for special considerations.)

Part-time Financial Controller

In order to balance the need for expertise with limited available funds, organizations often hire a financial controller on a part-time basis. This individual may work for him- or herself and have more than one client, or may be a contract employee with an accounting practice or a temporary work firm. Whatever the arrangement, there will be unique issues to be addressed in order for the financial controller to balance an arm's length involvement with the need to provide services equivalent to those a full-time financial controller would normally deliver. This section explores some of the steps a part-time financial controller should take to establish the expectations of the owners and to create appropriate terms of reference.

Expectations

Time constraints will be even more critical for a part-time financial controller, and it is therefore vital that priorities be clearly established by the owner and/or key managers alongside the part-time financial controller.

This will involve deciding precisely what core tasks must be completed. Financial controllers must exercise caution in order to avoid taking on a level of responsibility that cannot be exercised within the time available. As an example, having a comprehensive grasp of internal control may well be an impossible task if the individual is visiting only one or two days a week.

A good approach is to segregate the role into three functions, decide which of them is critical, and how much time should be allotted for each area. These are:

- project-based tasks (e.g., establishing a management reporting system, carrying out a risk analysis in order to establish the needs for insurance coverage, etc.);

- routine reporting tasks (e.g., working with staff to extract the monthly trial balance, review the results, prepare management reports, and indicate to management the areas to be addressed);

- business analyst and consultancy aspects (e.g., investigating issues raised by the organization's financial management practices — apparent cost over-runs, receivables delays, etc.).

The financial controller should be able to assess the amount of time required for each of these activities based on the state of the organization. As an example, the quality of the basic bookkeeping and the complexity of the financial system will determine the amount of time required to carry out the monthly closing and to generate the reports. If the financial controller fails to agree with company representatives on what the priorities are, there will likely be a gap between management's expectations on one part and the ability of the financial controller to deliver the anticipated results on the other. Worse still, problems could arise from the financial controller accepting a predetermined level of professional liability and not being able to carry out an adequate level of work to support the commitment.

Finally, the expectations to clarify must include not only which priorities to focus on but also the commercial and working arrangements that will apply, including:

- terms of reference for work content (as discussed above):

  ➤ a list of tasks the financial controller is to be responsible for,

  ➤ any projects with start and finish dates;

- level of authority and responsibility (i.e., to what extent will the financial controller act on behalf of the organization and be a part of company management?);

- expected presence/attendance at the organization's physical location (availability);

- agreement on any off-site work to be carried out;

- limitations (if required) on the minimum and maximum time availability, and provisions for requesting additional work;

- timing of specific deliverables (e.g., monthly financial reports);

- payment terms (both daily or retainer rates and payment due dates);

- methodology for handling problems or disputes (including withdrawal of services for non-payment);

- any liability disclaimers (e.g., a disclaimer concerning the financial controller's reliance on management's good faith, full disclosure of material information, and veracity of information provided, etc.);

- term of agreement and renewal/cancellation options;

- clauses to clarify the arm's length relationship as an independent party (possibly using the Canada Revenue Agency's guidelines, RC 4110, on defining employment/subcontractor roles).

While there could be some resistance to dealing with these "details" early in the relationship, experience shows that investing a small amount of time at the outset to clarify activities and responsibilities may well avoid significant problems at a later date.

Part-time financial controllers should also avoid two potential pitfalls: The first is "scope creep" where an initial agreement gradually gets added to, one small task at a time, until the financial controller realizes too late that the work required couldn't possibly fit into the time available. The second pitfall is under-pricing one's services as a part-time financial controller. The savings to the company should come from not committing to full-time employment rather than acquiring a "cheaper" financial controller. In fact, the rule of thumb is that there is generally a premium to be paid when a part-time commitment is made.

Staff responsibilities and communications

In defining roles and responsibilities, the financial controller should pay particular attention to his or her duties concerning staff selection, hiring, management, and, if required, terminations. Controllers should generally include performing regular staff reviews and providing feedback on performance, and the part-time financial controller should ensure, at the beginning of the assignment, that his or her involvement in such matters is communicated in writing to all staff so that there is no misunderstanding. Nothing is worse for employees than not clearly understanding for whom they work and to whom they are accountable. Also, how successfully the part-time financial controller carries out the job will depend heavily on the capability and performance of support staff, such as clerical workers. Their skills should be ascertained before time commitments are agreed upon.

The financial controller should pay special attention to establishing clear communication routines with staff. For example, issues that arise when he or she is not on site should be recorded so that they can be dealt with later. Recommendations in the communication area would include:

- establishing "get to know you" meetings before and at the beginning of the assignment;

- organizing one-on-one meetings with staff members to clarify their concerns and expectations;

- creating and confirming specific roles and responsibilities for all staff;

- setting up a perpetual "issues list" that staff can keep updating and is reviewed at each visit;

- setting up one-hour group sessions, at least once every two weeks, to deal with current issues;

- establishing an "emergency" method for staff to communicate problems that arise suddenly (including access to the financial controller via e-mail, cell phone, etc.).

The financial controller should recognize that this approach may be "abused" initially with seemingly insignificant issues being raised. However, this time should be viewed as a settling-in period to allow staff to become comfortable with the support they will receive from the new controller and with the openness of the relationship that is being created.

Other relationships

The part-time financial controller will have to ensure that his or her role is fully understood both internally and externally. The following measures are highly recommended:

- Provide written notice of the financial controller's appointment to all key contacts, and include a section that defines the scope of the position;

- Arrange a meeting with all key managers and supervisors in attendance as an opportunity to discuss the role, and to share expectations and current concerns;

- Establish a system to maintain and foster relationships with key managers (the management team) which includes an agreement that the part-time financial controller will attend all key planning sessions, etc.;

- Schedule regular meetings comprising the financial controller and the management team (e.g., a monthly review of financial results);

- Create an "advisory" role for the financial controller, whereby other managers can contact him or her to deal with issues and concerns that fall under the pre-established mandate.

The part-time financial controller has far less time to build personal relationships with his or her management peers, so every opportunity should be taken to have all parties work together to increase their mutual understanding.

Summary — do's and don'ts

- DO ensure that initial agreements are in place and that they are clear and concise;

- DO NOT under-price or over-extend your commitment;

- DO NOT take on accountability that you cannot provide;

- DO ensure that you have insurance coverage for this type of work;

- DO expect to have to work hard to build relationships;

- DO NOT accept company benefits as this will create problems with the arm's length compensation commitments;

- DO remain vigilant concerning potential control problems and ethical issues that may arise;

- DO communicate clearly on a regular basis;

- DO expect to receive payment on a regular basis.

Following these guidelines will help you to build a successful and rewarding career as a part-time financial controller. In a progressive and growing organization, this job could potentially turn into a full-time position.

Financial Controller of a New SME

Occasionally, situations arise where a financial controller has the opportunity to participate in a completely new venture. In a start-up situation, there will be no systems, no structures, and no processes in place — and most importantly, there will be very limited resources to carry out the accounting activity.

Yes, this can be a "once in a lifetime" opportunity to create a company's structure from scratch, but, for lack of resources, the financial controller may not be in a position to delegate tasks or hire consultants. He or she must then be prepared to participate in a broad range of tasks, from making bank deposits to developing strategic plans, and he or she will require a higher level of skill and knowledge in a number of areas.

"Infancy" phase

As the financial controller of an SME in the first days of start-up, you may not even have access to a telephone or desk. Here are some of the activities you should prepare to focus on as the business matures through the five stages of growth mentioned in the introduction:

- Start by creating an effective business plan. A key item to determine will be the organization's financing needs during start-up.

- Get a petty cash fund up and running. Most early activities will require quick access to cash.

- Establish relationships with key sources of finances. This may involve the securing of initial financing (a task beyond the scope of this guide). At the very least, banking relationships must be put in place to cover day-to-day activities.

- Decide how the first few staff members are going to be paid. Using a payroll processing bureau, such as a bank, is usually the only practical method.

- Set up a flexible chart of accounts that can be adapted as the business grows, preferably one that can be expanded on a modular basis.

- Put processes in place to deal with purchasing, payments and shipping, and billing. Establishing these processes early will be critical to ensuring that basic controls are in place. You can usually accomplish much of this work by creating batch lists to be filled in by others as the work happens and then posted on a summary basis.

- Plan on manually signing most cheques initially. This will allow you to quickly determine who your suppliers will be and will also provide you with an opportunity to negotiate terms.

- Focus primarily on cash flow management and planning. This is the activity that will make or break the company in this start-up phase.

"Childhood" or the early years of the business

This stage is entered when the business is under way and activity levels are increasing to the point where no one individual can manage all the processes. The following are some of the activities that you should concern yourself with at this stage:

- Hire support staff, usually a part-time bookkeeper first, who will carry out much of the routine data entry;

- Acquire computer modules for purchasing, inventory, and order entries/billing, rather than making do with manual systems;

- Upgrade the organization's financing based on the evolving needs of the business, looking at "layering" your funding sources to match balance sheet structures. Try a combination of the following tools:

  ➤ equity (through additional ownership funding, private placements, or other such sources),

  ➤ short-term debt (based on the company's ability to pay off and/or its projected ability to replace short-term debt with longer-term debt, say in 2-3 years),

  ➤ long-term debt for complementing equity, to the level justified by debt ratios and coverage ability;

- Work with the owners to help them establish their own financial plans in such a way as to complement their own tax planning and their longer-term needs — e.g., do succession planning, ensuring that shareholder agreements are in place, etc.;

- Carry out an initial risk assessment to identify what areas of the business should be addressed to protect the firm's ability to grow within a controlled and managed environment.

"Adolescence" or the phase when the business takes off

In many cases, achieving this phase will take a number of years. By this time, basic processes should be in place for handling a growing number of transactions with only limited growth in staff. Financing will be in place, and the focus will be on monitoring and control. The financial controller should, at this stage, be concentrating on providing support to management, knowing that the "back office" processes are in place. Key procedures should be documented and routinely followed, staff should be trained as needed, and the financial controller should be focusing solely on internal control and management of the processes, and have only limited "accounting" tasks to carry out.

Financial Controller in a Family-Run Business

In theory, a family-run business should be no different from any other. Each business has customers, suppliers, staff, and equipment. The need to obtain financing, control costs, and manage all other aspects should be exactly the same. Yet anyone who has been exposed to a family-run business, large or small, knows that this is not the case. The dynamics are vastly different, and they influence a broad range of business aspects, including how the organization is financed, where the offices are located, who manages what area of the business, who is hired and fired, what can be changed, and what is "sacrosanct".

The financial controller entering a family-run SME must be prepared for a new and different environment. Not only will there be the regular aspects of an SME — most of which have been covered in this guide — but he or she will also have to factor in the needs and desires of family members. Aspects to consider include the following:

BUSINESS ASPECT	IMPACT IN A FAMILY-CONTROLLED ENVIRONMENT
Financing	Will involve family members' personal wealth (in many cases, the family-run business is where most of their "net worth" resides). Debt is often linked to family guarantees. Often, there will be short- and long-term loans between family members and the business.

BUSINESS ASPECT	IMPACT IN A FAMILY-CONTROLLED ENVIRONMENT
Disclosure of financial data	Usually closely guarded, which inhibits the ability of the controller to know all of the relevant aspects concerning the business, while still binding him or her to careful protection of the financial information.
Salaries and management fees	The size of the salaries paid is often driven by a desire to get money out of the business. In many cases, figures may be out of line with market values and can potentially create internal problems and inequities.
Client relationships	Often based on a close relationship with family members, and existing as a number of "side deals" and deviations from accepted practices.
Supplier relationships	Also based on a close relationship with family members, which may limit the financial controller's ability to change suppliers because of high pricing or other problems, without involving the family in the process.
Expense control	The family will often buy personal items "through the business", inflating company costs and creating possible deductibility problems for taxation, not to mention difficulty in controlling, say, travel costs.
Insurance and risk management	Since they are the direct owners of the business, the amount of risk tolerated by the firm will be directly controlled by the owners' acceptance of "personal" risk.
Equity	Transfers of shares between family members can have a significant impact on control and decision making in the business.
Politics	Family members talk to each other about the business any time, day or night. This can be frustrating as decisions are often made by the immediate family members without consulting the firm's outside business advisors. This may also create problems that will require a sensitive touch to resolve.
Ethics	Often an area that requires continuous and close monitoring because of the thin line between a "theoretically" stand-alone corporation and the family members who personally own it. They may consider it their business only as to what actions are taken.

Family-owned businesses are unique in that the tone or culture of the business is set by those who own and run it. This underlying set of values determines expectations, not only in the approach to ethics, but also in all aspects of behaviour: how the organization treats clients and customers, staff, and suppliers; how it is committed to being part of the community and making "socially" based contributions; how the organization approaches managing risk and making investment decisions; as well as how the organization sees its responsibility in areas like environmental management. As the family business grows, these behavioural issues will need to be sustained. The impact on the controller is that such values form the basis of underlying approaches to policy development, and procedural and controls implementation. One function of the controller in such organizations may be to work with owners and incoming managers to ensure the sustainability of such values as the organization moves forward.

The above list is not exhaustive but it serves to illustrate the degree to which ownership threads its way through the organization to influence almost every aspect of the family-run business. Financial controllers must be sensitive to this impact. Although they are not family members, they often become privy to family matters in the course of performing their jobs. This may happen very gradually as the family begins to trust the individual with increasingly sensitive data, but the financial controller should always remember that he or she is (usually) not part of the family and therefore maintain a certain level of objectivity concerning this fact. For example, decisions may be taken that make little sense to an "outsider", but must stand based on the owners' prerogative and the influence of family members.

The qualities of trust, confidentiality, discretion, and sensitivity to the personal needs of the family members in such a business will often rank as important as any technical skills that the financial controller may bring to the table. As a last point, there is one cardinal rule to remember: never, ever create a situation where, as an independent third party, you find yourself caught in the middle of a family disagreement. State your position, be objective, and leave the issue for the family to resolve.

Appendix I: References

Financial controllers of SMEs should continually develop their networks and sources, as they will often be asked to investigate topics that are not familiar to them. In today's information-based society, there is significant value in knowing where to access information rather than trying to keep answers on hand at all times. In this section, we will identify some key resources and tools that may be helpful to financial controllers in building their bank of references and sources.

Computer-Based Sources

For the financial controller, the Internet is one of the most powerful sources of information. However, because the information it provides is so rapidly changing, any list written today could be outdated tomorrow. The following recommended resources should therefore not be considered complete. Some key Web sources are:

- professional accounting associations;

- other professional associations (e.g., insurance, actuarial, etc.);

- banks and other financial institutions;

- local boards of trade and chambers of commerce;

- most municipal, provincial, and federal government sites (in most countries);

- statistical bodies (government statistics, for example);

- many service providers (use a search engine to identify your search parameters);

- local, national, and international libraries; and

- major publishing houses and specialty publishers.

On a regular basis, financial controllers should invest time in searching the Internet in key areas of interest and then bookmark good references in the "favourites" tab for future consultation.

Publications and Services

Although most organizations that publish information now have Web sites, some financial controllers may want to have access to hard-copy materials such as books and loose-leaf offerings from publication services. The fastest way to contact these organizations is often through their Web site. Some of the publishers listed below may be of particular interest to financial controllers. CCH Canadian and Thomson Carswell are traditional loose-leaf service providers. John Wiley & Sons and Pearson are better known as suppliers of trade and technical publications.

- CCH Canadian Limited at 1-800-268-4522 or www.cch.ca

- John Wiley & Sons Canada Limited at 1-800-567-4797

- Pearson Canada at 1-800-567-3800

- Thomson Carswell at 1-800-387-5164

It is recommended that the financial controller also regularly consult the key trade publications related to the industry in which he or she is operating. Trade publications provide a powerful source for keeping up to date on issues, trends, and other topics that a financial controller should be conversant with in providing advice to a business.

Discussion Groups and Networking

The financial controller should establish a personal plan for networking and professional development. This plan should include items such as the following:

- Create a strategic career plan and identify the key skills and capabilities you will need. Use this information to:

  ➢ choose topics for your continuing professional education plan,

  ➢ identify and attend at least one industry or trade conference each year, or

  ➢ attend either a provincial or a national accounting association convention each year;

- While attending conferences and chapter events, identify business associates in positions similar to yours, and establish ongoing contact to address professional issues that may occur; and

- Take an active part in serving on an accounting or trade association committee to develop contacts and increase your awareness and skill levels.

Experience shows that many financial controllers, especially those in SMEs in similar positions, have encountered many of the issues you are or will be facing. Creating a network of such contacts with whom to discuss issues while maintaining confidentiality is an excellent way to save valuable time and increase your personal productivity.

Finally, the financial controller should maintain a contacts file or database, listing key contacts. This file should include the names of all existing service providers, key staff, and the resource people who can be contacted when specific issues arise.

Appendix II: Exhibits

Time data collection sheet for tracking time allocations

Where my time goes and what I need to change

Where my time goes	Happy?		If "No" action plan to change
	Yes	No	

Exhibit 1-A

Time planning sheet for assigning time to high priorities

Set targets and plan to move towards them

Current activities	Current time	Planned time	Action plan for change

Exhibit 1-B

Summary SWOT analysis

Strengths, Weaknesses, Opportunities, and Threats

Strengths	Opportunities
•	•
•	•
•	•
•	•
•	•
•	•
Weaknesses	**Threats**
•	•
•	•
•	•
•	•
•	•
•	•

Note that the template indicates up to six items in each category. Organizations should strive to arrive at this "Key Success Factors" and "Key Issues" type of priority list; however, this could start with a much longer list generated through a brainstorming session.

Exhibit 2-A

SWOT analysis worksheet

Strengths, Weaknesses, Opportunities, and Threats: Planning for action

Strengths		
Weaknesses		
	Threats	**Opportunities**

In this variation of the SWOT analysis, the planning worksheet can be used to start answering planning questions as follows:

- What are we going to do to address Threats with Strengths?

- What Opportunities can we exploit with our Strengths?

- What Weaknesses pose our greatest Threats and what is our action?

- What Opportunities can be addressed from our apparent Weaknesses?

Exhibit 2-B

Glossary of planning terminology

Possible scenario with examples

Name	Content/Purpose	Term	Example
Goal	An overall statement of where the organization intends to go.	Long term/high "organizational" level — usually maintained as a common purpose — strongly supports/complements/mirrors a mission/vision statement.	Our goal is total customer satisfaction; being the supplier of choice through leadership in customer service, quality products, competitive pricing, and strong partnerships with our suppliers.
Objective	A measurable milestone along the journey to achieve the organizational goal.	Medium term/high "organizational" level — may cover one, two, or even three years but supports current levels of activity.	To achieve an 85% CSR by year end 2009.
Strategy	One or more approaches through which a measurable objective will be decomposed and converted into work, accountability, and measurable progress indicators.	Short/medium term level — will probably mainly cover the core work for the upcoming plan period.	Contract Review — achieve a 100% right first time delivery against contract.
Plan	A breakdown of each strategy that will define how the strategy is to be implemented.	Short/medium term defining what work is being done and by whom.	This will break down into several elements, such as: People plans (training, hiring, education); Process plans (quality improvements, modifications, simplification, changes to standard terms); Tools — new system, system changes.

Exhibit 2-C

Name	Content/Purpose	Term	Example
Action	The "single line item" breakdowns within the plan that provide linkage to action "ownership" and which are measurable.	Actions are usually the key building blocks for individual performance agreements.	This is who does what, and will be the specific actions that individuals will take in order to implement the plans and deliver results.
Learning	The feedback loop through which effective performance measures at the objectives, strategy, plan, and action levels are reviewed.	Creates a basis for building a "learning" organization where experience is fed back and updates the planning cycle.	This will be driven from the creation of a management capacity to learn. How will the strategies, plans, and actions be monitored, and how will the learning be used to feed back to a continual improvement process? Tasks would be a) to create measures of anticipated outcomes and activity in order to monitor as work proceeds, and b) to define what the management process is to use this information.

Exhibit 2-C

Risk assessment checklist

Summary risk evaluation profile

No.	Area of exposure	Risk level	What is in place	What is the risk	What action is to be taken
	In this section we would place the item identified as a risk from the assessment exercise. The number (#) in the first column would just be as a reference for later discussion.		This would identify what, if any, action is currently in place to address this issue.	This would identify the possible risk of not taking further action (and could relate back to the risk tolerance area).	This would identify in summary form the possible actions that could be taken to address this gap.

Note that the risk level could be a numeric score developed through a matrix that compares impact of risk and potential occurrence. This would allow the organization to set priorities for action.

Exhibit 2-D

Process planning worksheet

PROCESS QUALITY PLAN

Process name:	Plan date:
Process step:	

Activity	Task	Potential risk of error	Risk			Action included in activity
			H	M	L	

Column	Explanation of use
Activity	Every process is made up of activities. This is the first level of analysis — what is the activity?
Task	Tasks are the things people do to complete an activity. For each activity there may be multiple tasks.
Potential risk of error	For most tasks things can go wrong. If we can identify them we can plan for them.
Risk	Based on the organization policy on and tolerance for risk, what is each risk classified as being?
Action included in activity	Given the risk identified, what action/control is built into the process to deal with it?

Exhibit 3-A

Cash-flow forecast sheet

Typical example of inflows and outflows

Ding-a-Ling Communications Inc.						
Cash-flow forecast worksheet						
Worksheet #2 sample inflow and outflow categories						
	January	**February**	**March**	**April**	**May**	**June**
Opening cash balance	$0	$0	$0	$0	$0	$0
Cash inflows						
Receivables						
Royalty receipts						
Legal settlements						
Total cash inflows	$0	$0	$0	$0	$0	$0
Cash outflows						
Payables — materials						
Payables — expenses						
Direct labour payroll						
Salaried payroll						
Source deductions						
Lease payments						
Rent payments						
Insurance premiums						
Shared cost advertising						
Professional/Legal fees						
Equipment/Capital purchase						
Income tax payments						
Total cash outflows	$0	$0	$0	$0	$0	$0
Net change in/(out)	$0	$0	$0	$0	$0	$0
Balance carried forward	$0	$0	$0	$0	$0	$0

Exhibit 3-B

Facilities management checklist

Question	Yes/No	Action Required
Land and Buildings		
1. Has a list been prepared of all buildings and land being occupied, whether rented, leased, or owned?		
2. Have all agreements associated with the rental, leasing, or ownership of the buildings and land been reviewed?		
3. Have all of the permits and licences associated with ownership and use of the buildings and lands been secured, and are they current?		
4. Have all agreements associated with building mechanics (air conditioning, heating, electrical, plumbing, snow removal, etc.) been reviewed?		
5. Have all agreements associated with servicing the buildings and land (utilities, garbage removal, landscaping, etc.) been reviewed?		
6. Have all agreements been analyzed for cost effectiveness, and are there opportunities to reduce costs or improve services?		
7. Have routine functions associated with the buildings and land been delegated to staff?		
8. Are there any opportunities to outsource functions to third parties?		
9. Are the current buildings and land adequate for the organization's plans for the next three years?		
Plant Equipment		
1. Has a list been prepared of all plant equipment that is rented, leased, or owned?		
2. Have all agreements associated with the rental, leasing, or ownership of the plant equipment been reviewed?		
3. Have all of the permits and licences associated with ownership and use of the plant equipment been secured, and are they current?		
4. Have all agreements associated with maintenance of the plant equipment been reviewed?		

Exhibit 3-C

Question	Yes/No	Action Required
5. Have all agreements been analyzed for cost effectiveness and are there opportunities to reduce costs, or increase capacity or quality?		
6. Have routine functions associated with plant equipment been delegated to staff?		
7. Are there any opportunities to outsource functions to third parties?		
8. Is the current plant equipment capacity adequate for the organization's plans for the next three years?		
Office and Computer Equipment		
1. Has a list been prepared of all office and computer equipment that is rented, leased, or owned?		
2. Have all agreements associated with the rental, leasing, or ownership of the office and computer equipment been reviewed?		
3. Have all agreements associated with maintenance of the office and computer equipment been reviewed?		
4. Have all agreements been analyzed for cost effectiveness and are there opportunities to reduce costs, or increase capacity or quality?		
5. Have routine functions associated with office and computer equipment been delegated to staff?		
6. Are there any opportunities to outsource functions to third parties?		
7. Is the current office and computer equipment capacity adequate for the organization's plans for the next three years?		
Office Services		
1. Has a list been prepared of all office services the organization has contracted for?		
2. Have all agreements associated with office services been reviewed?		

Exhibit 3-C

Question	Yes/No	Action Required
3. Have all agreements been analyzed for cost effectiveness and are there opportunities to reduce costs, or increase capacity or quality of service?		
4. Have routine functions associated with office services been delegated to staff?		
5. Are there any opportunities to outsource functions to third parties?		
6. Are the current office services adequate for the organization's plans for the next three years?		
Company Vehicles		
1. Has a list been prepared of all company vehicles?		
2. Have all agreements associated with company vehicles been reviewed?		
3. Have all agreements been analyzed for cost effectiveness and are there opportunities to reduce costs, or increase capacity or quality?		
4. Are all vehicles secured during business and non-business hours?		
5. Have the policies and procedures related to the use of company vehicles been reviewed?		
6. Are there procedures in place to record the utilization of vehicles in a manner that will satisfy tax regulations?		
7. Have the routine functions associated with company vehicles been delegated to staff?		
8. Are there any opportunities to outsource functions to third parties?		
9. Is the current fleet of company vehicles adequate for the organization's plans for the next three years?		

Exhibit 3-C

Skill set inventory

SKILL SET	PERSONAL ASSESSMENT	ACTION PLAN (IF REQUIRED)
Personal qualities: • positive attitude • integrity • trustworthiness/ confidentiality • emotional maturity • interest in the business • responsibility/leadership • commitment/desire to "get on board" with company's philosophy		
Management capabilities: • good listener/ communicator • effective organizer/ planner • good delegator • good "time manager" • responsive • good at change management • can relate to entrepreneurs		
Technical skills: • broad business knowledge • strategic thinking • operational knowledge • broad accounting skills • analytical strength • good presentation skills • basics of HR management • basics of IT management		

Exhibit 4-A

Accounting planning schedule

Date Due	Report/Process	Primary Responsibility	Back-Up Responsibility	Process Reference or Procedure

Exhibit 4-B

New controller — initial checklist

- Before day one, review the checklist and fill in those items already covered during the interview.

- In the first two days, define who you must talk to and create a plan to complete the inventory.

- Target having your checklist completed within the first 20 days.

- Review the checklist on a regular basis to identify potential areas of misunderstanding.

Area under Observation	Findings	Action Y/N
Owners' and key managers' concerns and expectations		
• What are the owners' expectations? • What is the company's vision/mission? • What is the preferred management style? — Frequent communications? Status reports? • Is there a job description for the controller? • What level of personal involvement is anticipated? • What information does the owner want? • What reporting is considered critical? • What areas are currently creating problems? • What plans are in place that will require financial commitments?		

Obligations and commitments that may already be in place		
• What contractual commitments are in place? E.g., ➢ auto/truck/equipment leases; ➢ service agreements (maintenance, elevators, office equipment, software support, telephones, postage metres, office services, etc.); ➢ management fee arrangements. • Are there any special obligations (royalty fees, licences, etc.)?		

Exhibit 7-A

AREA UNDER OBSERVATION	FINDINGS	ACTION Y/N
• Does the bank have a copy of the financial plans to assist in carrying out their performance measurement on the company?		

External relationships		
• What are the legal and contractual arrangements that the controller should be aware of? ➢ What banks are involved? ➢ Who are the contact persons? ➢ What agreements are in place? ➢ What is their status? ➢ What reporting is required? ➢ Who is the company secretary? ➢ Who keeps the minutes books, etc., and where?		
• Auditing, accounting, tax planning, and management issues, etc. ➢ Has a review been completed by the controller of the last management letters? ➢ Who are the audit contacts? ➢ Do the auditors have any concerns? ➢ What tax planning is done and by whom? ➢ Is tax planning linked to the owners' personal tax? ➢ What is the status of the last year end? ➢ What is the status of tax returns and payments? ➢ Are instalments being paid on time? ➢ Has the controller done a review of the latest tax assessments/returns?		
• Supply arrangements and relationships that may be in place: ➢ What materials are critical for the company? ➢ Who are the key suppliers of these materials? ➢ Have there been any problems with procurement, quality, delivery, etc.?		

Exhibit 7-A

AREA UNDER OBSERVATION	FINDINGS	ACTION Y/N
➤ Are payments up to date? Are there any disputes? ● Are there any risks associated with suppliers?		

Job function issues		
● Processing issues — What processes are in place? Who does what tasks? ➤ What staff members are in place? ➤ What is their experience and skills level? ➤ Are the responsibilities defined by the individual? ➤ Who is responsible for each key accounting function (billing, payables, etc.)? ➤ Who are the signing officers? ➤ Is there petty cash, and who is responsible for it? ➤ Is purchasing controlled and by whom? ➤ Is cash tracked on a daily basis and by whom? ➤ Are all AR write-offs approved? ➤ Have discounts been reviewed and all taken? ➤ Have all miscellaneous amounts adjusted been reviewed?		
● Reporting issues — What reports are generated? By whom? For whom? When? ➤ What reports are created by staff? — internal management reports, — reports for the owners/Board, — reports for the bank, line of credit, etc., — other reports. ➤ When are reports due? What are the deadlines? ➤ Is there a schedule of items produced? ➤ Are they being created on time? ➤ Have they been reviewed for "user value"? ➤ What budgets, plans, or forecasts exist?		

Exhibit 7-A

Area under Observation	Findings	Action Y/N
• Are they timely to allow effective action?		

Customers		

• Who are the key customers? Where are they? What is their history?
  ➢ Who are the key customers?
    — internal customers/users,
    — external customer "bank", etc.,
    — "real" customers of the business.
  ➢ Where are they located?
  ➢ What percentage of sales do they each account for?
  ➢ What is their payment record?
  ➢ Are there current problems?
  ➢ Are there any outstanding credits due?
  ➢ Are there discount programs in place?
  ➢ Are there special relationships (e.g., with the owners)?
  ➢ What is the order backlog?
  ➢ What is the trend of backlog?
  ➢ Are items being shipped as required and on time?
  ➢ What details are known about product/customer margins?		

Administration		

• Office management arrangements;
  ➢ Who is responsible for:
    — equipment,
    — telephone systems,
    — photocopier machines,
    — fax machines,
    — mobile phones/other communications,
    — mailing/mail room equipment,
    — postage meters/systems;
  ➢ What equipment does the company own?
  ➢ What leases are in place?		

Exhibit 7-A

Area under Observation	Findings	Action Y/N
➢ Are maintenance agreements in place? ➢ What problems are being encountered? ➢ Who manages the changes to telephone systems? ➢ Who is responsible for janitorial services, coffee, vending machines, and trash? ➢ Who is responsible for office supplies? ➢ Who is responsible for facilities, leases, etc.? ➢ Who looks after building maintenance? ➢ Who looks after security (regular/off hours)? ➢ Does the company use office layout contractors? ➢ Are there policies or procedures in place covering administration issues?		

• Computers
➢ Who is responsible for computers?
  — hardware,
  — software,
  — networks/communications?
➢ Is there a company Web site?
➢ Who maintains it/approves data?
➢ Who manages the e-mail systems?
➢ Is there Internet access? How is it used?
➢ Who is responsible for data communications?
➢ Are back-ups of data done? By whom and when?
➢ What software is being used?
➢ Is it controlled or standardized?
➢ Is the software licensed or does the firm use original versions?
➢ Are there support agreements in place?		

Exhibit 7-A

AREA UNDER OBSERVATION	FINDINGS	ACTION Y/N
Human resources administration		
• Are there documented HR policies and procedures?		
• Are there written employee agreements related to procedures or to confidentiality of data?		
• Is there a union or collective agreement?		
• Are there any HR concerns or unrest?		
• Has an employee survey been conducted?		
• How is new hiring approved?		
• Are outside recruitment agencies used?		
• Who is responsible for pay rates or reviews?		
• Who processes payroll?		
• What benefit plans are in place?		
• Who are the carriers?		
• Are there any benefits advisors contracted?		
• Where are pay arrangements defined (e.g., overtime, shift allowance, etc.)?		
• Are there special allowances (e.g., travel, etc.)?		
• Are there policies on harassment and other special situations?		
Other key areas to address		
• What steps are in place to identify/handle job stress and personal problems?		
• Are guidelines and policies such as Workers' Compensation being adhered to?		
• Is there a Health and Safety committee?		
• Is first aid equipment in place and maintained?		
• Are fire drills conducted on a regular basis?		

Exhibit 7-A

Other special observations, issues or concerns

TOPICAL INDEX